THE COMPLETE GUIDE TO
WORLD RECORDS

Sandy Creek
NEW YORK

An Imprint of Sterling Publishing
387 Park Avenue South
New York, NY 10016

ISBN: 978-1-4351-4410-1 (print format)

A CIP record for this book is available from the Library of Congress.

For information about custom editions, special sales, and premium and corporate purchases, please contact Sterling Special Sales at 800-805-5489 or specialsales@sterlingpublishing.com.

Manufactured in China
Lot #:
10 9 8 7 6 5 4 3 2 1
09/12

Picture Credits

Key: bg = background, l = left, r = right, t= top, m = middle, b = bottom.

THE COMPLETE GUIDE TO
WORLD
RECORDS

KENNY CLEMENTS

Sandy Creek
NEW YORK

CONTENTS

Largest man-made structure
Page 50

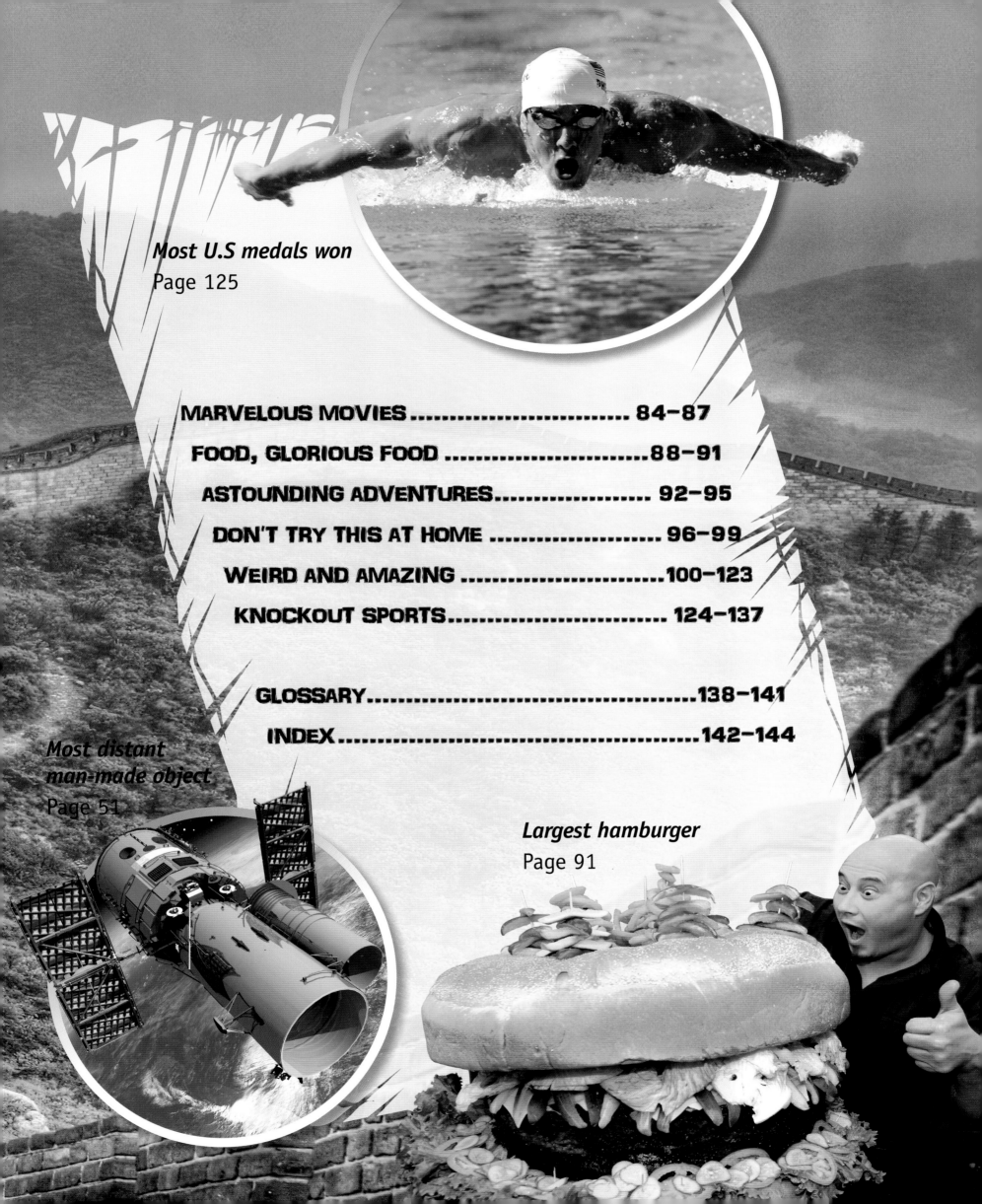

Most U.S medals won
Page 125

Most distant man-made object
Page 51

Largest hamburger
Page 91

INTRODUCTION

Widest tornado
page 17

Since the ancient Greeks held the very first Olympic Games, people have pushed themselves to be the fastest, the strongest, the very best that they can be. This desire to break new records is not limited to sports, however. People have been striving to be the first to invent new and wonderful things since humans first walked on our planet: the first wheel, the first automobile, the first jet airplane, the first trip to the Moon.

They want to conquer the tallest mountain, descend to the depths of the deepest cave, identify the loudest animal, discover the smallest creature, construct the tallest building, even collect the most salt and pepper!

Tallest man alive
page 10

Largest country
page 58

Oldest fossils
page 45

This book is a celebration of many of the world's most important records, both natural and man-made. From the biggest tree in the world to the most active volcano. From the deepest lake to the farthest planet. From the oldest creature to the smallest man.

It honors some of the greatest inventors, athletes, and pioneers in construction, science, and engineering, but this book is also a guide to the amazing, and often very strange or amusing, achievements of ordinary people who have extraordinary features, skills, talents, collections, or pastimes.

This is a guide to our wonderful planet, our **solar system**, and, above all, the part of human nature that wants to recognize, and be recognized as, the world's best. This is the Complete Guide to World Records.

Heaviest insect
page 18

WHERE IN THE WORLD?

ARCTIC OCEAN

NORTH AMERICA

This is the most crowded city in the US...
page 59

The fastest man in the world lives here...
page 133

ATLANTIC OCEAN

6

7

2

A man from here ate a whole airplane...
page 100

1

PACIFIC OCEAN

3

CENTRAL AMERICA

4

The most active volcano in the world is here...
page 45

5

The oldest creatures on the planet live here...
page 39

The world's tallest waterfall is here...
page 11

THE TALLEST

Tallest man alive

The tallest man alive is Sultan Kösen of Turkey, in Western Asia. Doctors helped him to stop growing when he reached 8 feet 3 inches tall. Sultan also has the largest hands (11.22 inches) and the largest feet (14.4 inches).

DID YOU KNOW? DID YOU KNOW? DID YOU KNOW? DID YOU KNOW?

The tallest dinosaur was Sauroposeidon. This huge creature had a very long neck and a small head and could stand nearly 60 feet tall!

Size 28 shoes, phew!

Tallest snow(wo)man

The townsfolk of Bethal, Maine, love the snow. They built a 113 feet 7 inches snowman, the world's tallest, in 1999. Then they broke their own record in 2008, when they built the world's tallest snow woman. She measured 122 feet 1 inch!

Tallest rollercoaster

The world's tallest rollercoaster is the 456-feet Kingda Ka, which scares the living daylights out of folks at Six Flags Great Adventure in Jackson, New Jersey. It was also the world's fastest ride until the Formula Rossa rollercoaster opened in Abu Dhabi, in the United Arab Emirates, in 2010.

Tallest totem pole

The world's tallest totem pole stands in McKinleyville, California. It is 160 feet tall and weighs 57,000 pounds. Totem poles are trees that have been carved to depict ancient legends and symbols.

Tallest waterfall

Angel Falls is the tallest waterfall on the planet, tumbling 3,212 feet down the Auyan Tepui mountain in Canaima National Park, Venezuela. It throws up so much spray that folks standing a mile away from it can still get wet!

THE SMALLEST

Smallest woman

The world's smallest woman is Jyoti Amge, who lives in Nagpor, India. She is just 2 feet 6 inches tall, but she hasn't let this bother her. She has big ideas and plans to be a politician. She is already the world's shortest election campaigner!

Smallest mammoth

The world's smallest mammoth (a mammoth was a woolly, prehistoric elephant) stood less than 4 feet tall. The bones of one were discovered on the island of Crete, in Greece. Fully grown, it was only about the size of a newborn elephant today!

Smallest horse

Thumbelina is the world's smallest horse. Standing just 17½ inches tall and weighing 60 pounds, the **miniature** chestnut-colored mare lives with her owners, the Goessling family, on a farm in Missouri. She is smaller than most of the farm dogs!

RECORD BREAKER

Mr. Peebles is the world's smallest cat. The tiny kitty is only 5.9 inches long and weighs 3 pounds. He lives with his very careful owner, Robin Svendson, in Illinois.

Smallest waist

The smallest waist in the world belongs to an American woman named Cathie Jung, from Old Mystic, Connecticut. Her natural waist measures 21 inches, but when she tightens her corset it becomes a tiny 15 inches! She really does look like an **hourglass**!

Cathie wears her corset 24 hours a day.

Smallest frog

The tiniest frog on the planet is smaller than an M&M! It is the 0.27 inch Paedophryne amauensis frog and it lives almost invisibly among the leaves on the floor of the rainforest in New Guinea, in the southwest Pacific Ocean.

This fully-grown mammoth is the same size as a baby elephant

THE LONGEST

DID YOU KNOW? DID YOU KNOW? DID YOU KNOW?

The longest serving U.S. president was Franklin D. Roosevelt, who was the 32nd President of the United States. He had the job for 12 years, 1 month, and 8 days.

Longest snake

The longest snake that ever **slithered** was the 45-foot Titanoboa. Luckily for us, it disappeared 58 million years ago! Today, the longest snake is a 25-foot python called Medusa. She lives at the Edge of Hell haunted house attraction in Kansas City.

Researchers have estimated that Titanoboa weighed about 2,500 pounds and measured about 3 feet in diameter at the thickest part of its body.

Longest nose

Mehmet Ozyurek of Artvin, Turkey, has the world's longest nose. It measures 3.46 inches from the bridge to the tip. That's a world record not to be sniffed at!

Longest hair

The lady with the longest hair is Xie Qiuping of China. Her locks are an astonishing 18 feet 5.54 inches. Her hair hasn't been cut since 1973, making her a real life Rapunzel.

Longest word

The longest word in the English **dictionary** has 45 letters! The word is neumonoultramicroscopicsilicovolcanoconiosis and is a translation of the Greek word for lung disease. That's a mouthful!

Longest reign

The longest **reigning** king of all time was Sobhuza II, the King of Swaziland, in southern Africa. He was ruler of his country for 82 years and 254 days, until his death in 1982. That's **dedication** to the job!

THE WIDEST

RECORD BREAKER

The Wandering Albatross has the world's widest wingspan. The sea bird's enormous wings can stretch up to 11 feet!

Widest mouth

The man with the widest mouth in the world is Francisco Domingo Joaquim from Angola in southern Africa. His mouth can stretch to 6½ inches across. It's so large, he can hold an entire soda can sideways in his mouth!

Widest tree

The world's widest tree covers 3½ acres of land near Calcutta, in India. It is the 250 year-old Great Banyan tree. At first glance it looks like a forest, but the "tree trunks" are really 2,800 of the banyan tree's roots that have grown above the ground!

Widest river

The widest river in the world is the Río de la Plata, which flows between Argentina and Uruguay in South America. It is 140 miles wide at its broadest section and covers 14,000 square miles. Río de la Plata is Spanish for "Silver River."

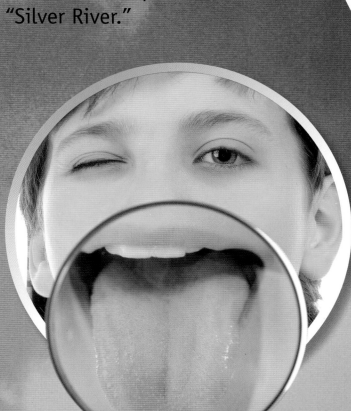

Widest tongue

The widest tongue belongs to Jay Sloot of Perth, Australia. His tongue is 3.1 inches at its widest point and it can lift an entire soda can!

Widest tornado

The widest tornado ever measured by **radar** was the Mulhall tornado that hit northern Oklahoma in 1999. It was 360 feet and 11 inches at its widest swirling point and caused damage up to 4 miles away from its epicenter!

THE HEAVIEST

Heaviest insect

The heaviest insect in the world is the giant weta, a type of cricket that lives in New Zealand. It is about the size of a man's hand and weighs 2.5 ounces, which is three times the weight of a mouse. Bizarrely, it enjoys eating carrots!

DID YOU KNOW? DID YOU KNOW? DID YOU KNOW?

The world's heaviest metal is iridium, which weighs about 33 pounds per cubic foot.

Heaviest production car

The heaviest car in production is the Maybach 62, which weighs 6,294 pounds. It's a luxury ride and costs around $400,000. Each car is customized for its owner, so every one is unique.

MAYBACH 62

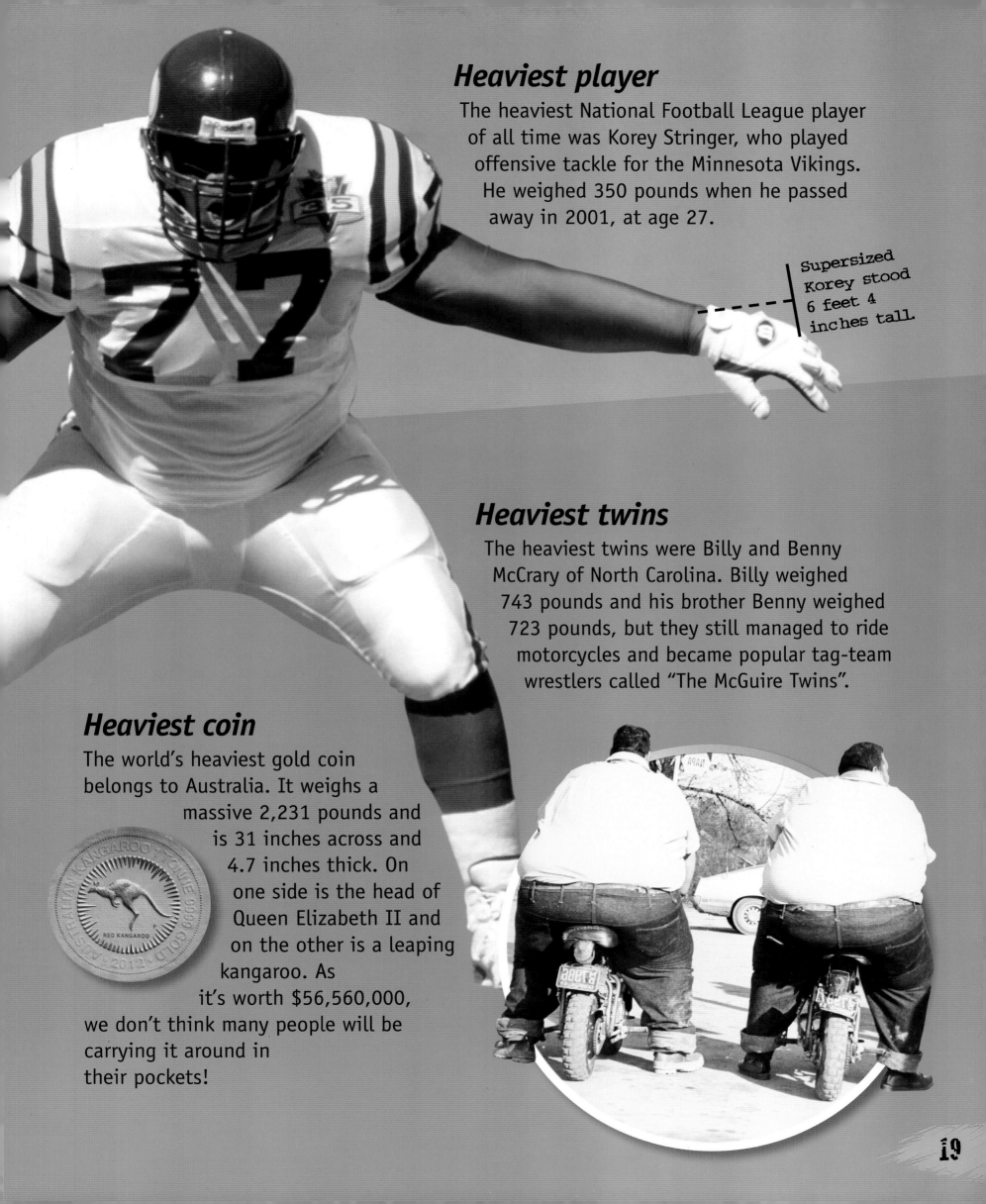

Heaviest player

The heaviest National Football League player of all time was Korey Stringer, who played offensive tackle for the Minnesota Vikings. He weighed 350 pounds when he passed away in 2001, at age 27.

Supersized Korey stood 6 feet 4 inches tall

Heaviest twins

The heaviest twins were Billy and Benny McCrary of North Carolina. Billy weighed 743 pounds and his brother Benny weighed 723 pounds, but they still managed to ride motorcycles and became popular tag-team wrestlers called "The McGuire Twins".

Heaviest coin

The world's heaviest gold coin belongs to Australia. It weighs a massive 2,231 pounds and is 31 inches across and 4.7 inches thick. On one side is the head of Queen Elizabeth II and on the other is a leaping kangaroo. As it's worth $56,560,000, we don't think many people will be carrying it around in their pockets!

THE MOST...

Most trips into space

U.S. software billionaire Charles Simonyi has made more trips into space as a tourist than any other person on Earth. He paid $55 million to spend a total of 29 days in space in 2007 and 2009. That's out of this world!

CHARLES SIMONYI
ЧАРЛЬЗ СИМОНИ

Animal with the most teeth

The land animal with the most teeth is the giant armadillo, which has 100. In the sea, the record-breaker is the long-snouted spinner dolphin, which has 252 teeth.

Most tattooed

The world's most tattooed person is Lucky Diamond Rich, a performance artist from New Zealand. His tattoos cover not only his entire body, but the inside of his mouth and ears as well! He makes his living by juggling chainsaws—scary!

Lucky Diamond Rich has spent over 1,000 hours under the tattooist's needle.

Most inventions

The British are credited with producing 54 percent of the world's most important inventions, making the UK the most inventive country on the planet. Did you know that Brits invented TV, radio, the computer, the World Wide Web, the telephone, the jet engine, the light bulb, plastic, cement, tarmac, and even the flushing toilet?

Most legs

The creature on Earth with the most legs is the millipede. "Mil" is the Latin word for "thousand" and "ped" is Latin for "feet." But a millipede only has 750 legs, not 1,000, as its name suggests!

THE HIGHEST

Highest bungee jump

The highest bungee jump in the world is from the Macau Tower in China. Jumpers **plummet** 764 feet at a terrifying 125 miles per hour before the cord (hopefully!) yanks them back into the air.

Highest IQ

The person with the highest ever IQ (Intelligence Quotient—that's how your brainpower is measured) is Marilyn vos Savant, of St. Louis, Missouri. The ultra-smart magazine columnist has an IQ of 228. The average IQ in the US is 98. Better get studying if you want to beat her!

Highest paid sportsman

The world's highest paid NFL player is Peyton Manning, quarterback for the Indianapolis Colts until March 2012. He made $500,000 per week during the football season! The highest earning soccer player is Lionel Messi from Argentina, who plays for FC Barcelona in Spain. He earns $916,667 a week!

Highest shoes

The world's highest-heeled shoes have an 11-inch platform and a 16-inch heel. They were made by a shoe company in Cheshire, England, UK, and cost over $1,100 a pair. They won't win any races!

Highest lake

The lake at the top of the world is the Ojos del Salado Pool in Argentina. At 20,965 feet, this pool of water lies in the crater of an active volcano!

THE FASTEST

Fastest computer

The world's fastest computer is the Tianhe-1A supercomputer, which was built in China. It can carry out 1,000 trillion operations every second. That's just mindboggling!

Fastest land speed

The world speed record on land is held by the British jet-propelled car Thrust SSC. This **supersonic** car, driven by Royal Air Force pilot Andy Green, broke the sound barrier in 1997 at a speed of 763 miles per hour, in Black Rock Desert, Nevada.

Fastest airplane

The fastest **unmanned** airplane in the world is NASA's X-43A Scramjet, which can reach 7,000 miles per hour in just 11 seconds. That's 9.3 times faster than the speed of sound!

Fastest train

The fastest train in the world is the French TGV. It set a new world record in 2007 when it reached a top speed of 357.2 miles per hour. *C'est magnifique*, as the French might say.

The TGV's top speed is roughly half the speed of sound.

Fastest police

Italian felons should just surrender when they hear the siren of the State Traffic Police. The Lamborghini Gallardo is the world's fastest police car, with a top speed of 192 miles per hour. Might as well pull over, as you'll never outrun these crimebusters!

THE FASTEST

Fastest spin

The fastest spin on ice skates was 308 turns in one minute! The lady with the spinning head was figure skater Natalia Kanounnikova from Russia. She set the record at the Rockefeller Center Ice Rink in New York in 2006.

Natalia started skating at just four years old.

Fastest feet

James Devine is officially the fastest dancer in the world. The Irishman is a champion dancer and **choreographer.** He managed to perform 39 taps per second in a dancing display in Sydney, Australia, in 1998.

Fastest guitarist

The world's fastest guitar player is John Taylor of Westminster, Colorado. The music teacher set a world record by playing composer Rimsky-Korsakov's *The Flight of the Bumblebee* at a **plectrum**-melting 600 beats per minute!

Fastest cutter

If your hair needs a quick trim, the fastest hairdresser in the world is Ivan Zoot from Chicago, Illinois. He holds the records for the fastest haircut (55 seconds), the most haircuts in 1 hour (34), and the most haircuts in 24 hours, non-stop (340)!

DID YOU KNOW? DID YOU KNOW? DID YOU KNOW? DID YOU KNOW?

The fastest **checkmate** in a game of chess is a series of moves known as "Fool's Mate."

Fastest followers

U.S. pop queen Lady Gaga became the first person ever to notch up 20 million followers on **Twitter** in March 2012. The superstar was also the first to hit 10 and 15 million followers. That's Gaga!

THE LOUDEST

Loudest explosion

When the volcanic island of Krakatoa, in Indonesia, erupted in 1883, the sound of the explosion could be heard 3,000 miles away. The eruption was so violent that it changed the world's weather for the next 5 years!

The lava that shoots out of a volcano is actually rock that has turned to liquid in the extreme heat.

Loudest burp

The world's loudest human burp escaped from a British man named Paul Hunn. His mega-burp registered 109.9 **decibels** in 2009. His mom must have been so proud!

Loudest purr

Smokey the cat has the loudest purr in the world. The British Shorthair cat, who lives with her owner Ruth Adams in Northampton, UK, can hit 67.7 decibels when she's feeling particularly happy. That's almost as loud as a lawnmower!

Loudest horn

A U.K. company has invented the world's loudest bicycle horn. "The Hornster" can be honked at a deafening 178 decibels if a car or pedestrian gets in the cyclist's way. That's about as loud as a 747 airplane taking off!

Loudest bullhorn

The world's loudest bullhorn was used to keep spectators in order at the 2012 Olympic Games in London. It can emit 150 decibels that can be heard two miles away!

RECORD BREAKER

The loudest sound ever heard was the **impact** explosion of a **meteor** from space crashing to Earth. It landed near the Podkamennaya Tunguska River in Krasnoyarsk Krai, Russia, on June 30, 1908.

AMAZING ANIMALS

Longest non-stop bird migration

The longest non-stop bird **migration** was by a bar-tailed godwit, which flew 7,145 miles from Alaska to New Zealand in nine days. Hope he had a good vacation when he got there...

Dorsal fin

Sailfish have a long, bony, spear-shaped bill, sometimes called a snout, beak, or rostrum. Like a true sword, it is smooth, flat, pointed, and sharp.

Fastest fish

The blue sailfish is the fastest fish in the ocean. It can swim at up to 68 miles an hour. It's called a sailfish because the large dorsal fin on top of its body looks just like a boat sail when it pokes above the water.

World's strongest creature

The world's strongest creature is the rhinoceros beetle. This little insect can carry 850 times its own body weight. It's a miniature **Hercules**!

The body of an adult rhinoceros beetle is covered by a thick exoskeleton.

DID YOU KNOW? DID YOU KNOW? DID YOU KNOW? DID YOU KNOW?

The world's newest ape is the northern buffed cheeked gibbon. Scientists only discovered the **species** living in a rainforest in Vietnam in 2010.

Greatest insect high jumper

The froghopper (sometimes called the spittle bug) is the insect world's greatest high jumper. The tiny 0.2-inch bug can clear more than 2 feet in one jump.

Greatest leaper

The African Impala (a type of antelope) can spring 10 feet into the air and leap 33 feet at a time. That's practically flying!

AMAZING ANIMALS

Best sense of smell

The "Best Sense of Smell Award" goes to the male emperor moth. He can smell a female moth from 7 miles away. That must be strong perfume!

Fastest animal

The fastest animal on Earth is the spotted cheetah, which lives in parts of Africa and the Middle East. It can reach 60–70 miles per hour in just three seconds when it's chasing prey. That's fast!

RECORD BREAKER

The largest wild dog of all time was the Epicyon, which once roamed the plains of North America. It was six times larger than a pet Labrador and weighed 225 pounds.

Fastest flier

The swiftest feathered flier is the peregrine falcon, which can flash across the sky at 200 miles an hour when it is swooping down to catch its dinner. Run, rabbit, run!

Farthest distance swum

The farthest distance ever swum by a mammal was a journey taken by a humpback whale. The giant whale swam 9,942 miles from Costa Rica to Antarctica. That's a long voyage!

Leatherbacks can stay underwater for up to 85 minutes.

Deepest reptile dive

The deepest recorded dive by a reptile was by a leatherback turtle. It can paddle down as far as ¼ of a mile beneath the sea.

AMAZING ANIMALS

DID YOU KNOW? DID YOU KNOW? DID YOU KNOW? DID YOU KNOW?

The spookfish, which swims in the northeast Pacific Ocean, has six eyes! Do you think it sees eye-to-eye with the other fish?

Largest tree-dwelling animal

The reddish-brown orangutan is the world's largest tree-dwelling animal. This giant ape weighs about 200 pounds and grows to 5 feet in height, but its arms can grow to 7 feet in length! Orangutans only live in Borneo and Sumatra and their name means "person of the forest."

Longest migration on foot

Instead of flying to warmer places in winter like most other birds, the North American quail walks there instead! These quails have been known to travel 5,000 feet up mountains to reach warmer spots. It's the longest migration by a bird on foot!

Rarest gorilla

The world's rarest gorilla was a giant albino called Little Snowflake. This magnificent white ape lived at a zoo in Barcelona, Spain, until he died of old age in 2003. Unlike most albinos, Little Snowflake had blue eyes instead of the normal pink eyes.

Hairiest crustacean

You've probably heard of the legendary yeti, but have you heard of the yeti lobster? This one is definitely real! It lives on the sea floor of the South Pacific Ocean and its limbs and claws are covered in blond fur! It is the world's hairiest **crustacean**.

The yeti lobster lives near deep, underwater geysers that are toxic to many creatures.

Biggest animal structures

North American beavers are responsible for building the biggest animal structures on the planet. Using mud, branches, and plants, the beavers construct homes (called lodges) in dams, which they create by blocking rivers to make still pools. The largest lodge ever found measured 40 feet across and was 16 feet high.

AMAZING ANIMALS

Most dangerous

The most dangerous creature on the planet isn't a lion or a shark, but the female Anopheles mosquito. This tiny insect carries malaria, a deadly disease that kills 1 million people every year. It lives mainly in Africa.

Only female mosquitoes bite. They suck blood because they need protein to produce their eggs.

Loudest animal

The loudest animal on land is the well-named howler monkey. Its screams can be heard from 3 miles away! It would have no trouble calling you in at bedtime.

Biggest horns

The water buffalo has the longest horns of any living animal. Its huge curved horns can grow up to 5 feet long. In some countries the horns are made into flutes and other musical instruments when the animal dies.

Most poisonous

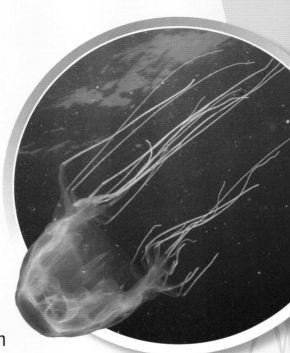

The sea wasp is the most poisonous jellyfish in the world. It has 60 tentacles, each about 10 feet long. It may sound like a creature from science fiction, but it exists. One sea wasp contains enough venom to kill 60 humans!

DID YOU KNOW? DID YOU KNOW? DID YOU KNOW? DID YOU KNOW?

The world's rarest big cat is the Amur leopard. Fewer than 35 are thought to still exist in China and Russia.

Largest animal

The largest animal ever known to have existed is the blue whale, which can grow to more than 98 feet in length and can weigh 200 tons. It is also the loudest sea mammal in the ocean. The whale's low-frequency whistle can reach 188 decibels, which can be heard hundreds of miles away underwater.

AMAZING ANIMALS

Largest living animal

The largest living animal on dry land is the African elephant, which can grow to 12 feet in height and weigh more than 13,000 pounds. You wouldn't want one to sit on your lap!

Tiniest bird

The tiniest bird in the world is the green and blue Cuban bee hummingbird. It only grows to 2 inches and weighs about 0.6 of an ounce. That's about the same weight as a penny. This bird is a real featherweight!

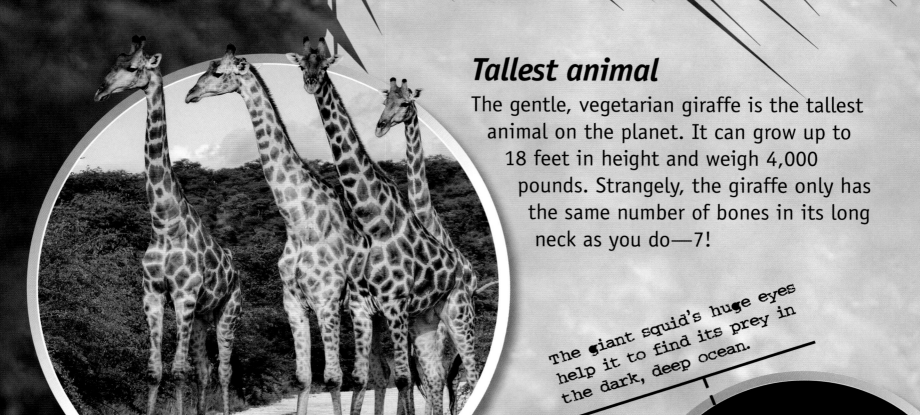

Tallest animal

The gentle, vegetarian giraffe is the tallest animal on the planet. It can grow up to 18 feet in height and weigh 4,000 pounds. Strangely, the giraffe only has the same number of bones in its long neck as you do—7!

The giant squid's huge eyes help it to find its prey in the dark, deep ocean.

Largest invertebrate

The world's largest invertebrate (that's an animal without a backbone) is the Giant Squid. Its 8 arms can grow up to 33 feet in length, it weighs nearly a ton and its eyes are as big as a human head! Very few people have seen a giant squid in real life, so it remains something of a mystery.

Longest living

The longest living creature on Earth was a Madagascar radiated tortoise, which was 188 years old when it died in 1965. Several giant tortoises on the Galapagos Islands, in the Pacific Ocean, have lived as long as 150 years.

NATURAL WONDERS

Longest living

The American tree that lives the longest is the Great Basin bristlecone pine, which grows high up in the White Mountains of California. You can tell how old a tree is by counting the rings on the inside of its trunk. When one fell down, the rings showed that it had lived for 4,844 years!

Oldest tree

The oldest tree in the world is a type of spruce that grows in the mountains in Sweden. The roots are 8,000 years old, but the stems are replaced every 600 years or so.

Tallest tree

The tallest tree ever discovered was a 379-foot and 1 inch coast redwood, which grew in Redwood National Park, California. It's a real giant beanstalk!

Largest leaves

The largest leaves on the planet belong to the raffia palm. This palm tree is found in Africa and its leaves can grow as long as 80 feet.

RECORD BREAKER

North America's biggest collection of carnivorous plants (that's plants that trap and eat insects and small animals), including Venus flytraps, is kept at California Carnivores plant nursery, near Sebastopol.

Heaviest wood

The heaviest wood comes from the black ironwood plant. It is a relative of the olive tree and grows in Florida and the Keys, and throughout Africa and the West Indies. Its wood is so heavy that, unlike most other types of wood, it does not float in water but sinks to the bottom.

NATURAL WONDERS

Deepest lake

The deepest lake is Lake Baikal in Russia, with a depth of 2,442 feet. It is also the world's oldest and is believed to be 25 million years old!

Deepest canyon

The deepest canyon on Earth isn't the Grand Canyon in Arizona, which is 6,000 feet deep. It's the Yarlung Tsangpo Grand Canyon in Tibet, which is part of China. The Tsangpo Canyon is 18,000 feet deep.

Deepest lake

The deepest lake is Lake Baikal in Russia, with a depth of 2,442 feet. It is also the world's oldest and is believed to be 25 million years old!

Most valuable natural jewel

The most valuable natural "jewel" is not amber or coral or jet, it is the coconut pearl. This rare pearl sometimes grows inside a coconut shell. If you smashed open one million coconuts you would be extremely lucky to find even one of these pearls! It is the most valuable because it is the most rare.

Hottest chili

The world's hottest chili pepper is the Morugo Scorpion, which grows in Trinidad and Tobago, in the southern Caribbean. This red-colored pepper is about the size of a golf ball.

Fastest melting

The fastest melting ice glacier, named Pine Island, is in Antarctica. Scientists are worried because the ice is melting very quickly and could make the sea level rise by 3 feet before the end of this century.

A recent crack in the glacier could create an iceberg the size of New York.

NATURAL WONDERS

Largest number of geysers

The largest number of geysers found in one place is in Yellowstone National Park, in Wyoming. Geysers are eruptions of hot water and steam that shoot out of the ground. There are at least 500 geysers in Yellowstone National Park and only around 1,000 worldwide. The most famous geyser at Yellowstone is called "Old Faithful."

Largest hailstone

The largest hailstone, or ice fall, crashed down on top of Ord, in Scotland, in 1849. It was a 20-foot ice monster called a "megacryometeor." The largest recorded hailstone to fall in the USA was 8 inches long and landed in Vivian, South Dakota, in 2010. It would still have given you a giant headache!

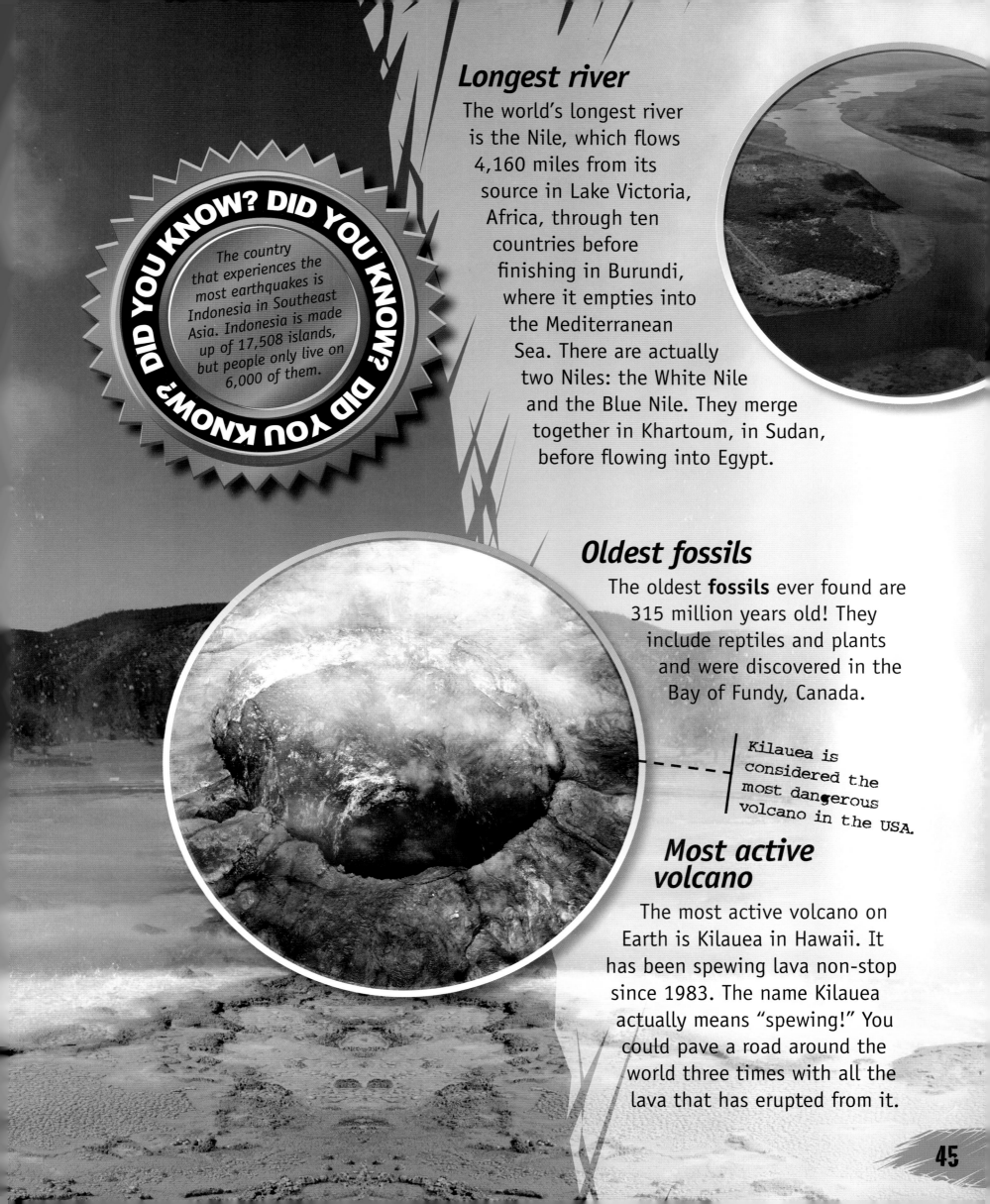

Longest river

The world's longest river is the Nile, which flows 4,160 miles from its source in Lake Victoria, Africa, through ten countries before finishing in Burundi, where it empties into the Mediterranean Sea. There are actually two Niles: the White Nile and the Blue Nile. They merge together in Khartoum, in Sudan, before flowing into Egypt.

Oldest fossils

The oldest **fossils** ever found are 315 million years old! They include reptiles and plants and were discovered in the Bay of Fundy, Canada.

Kilauea is considered the most dangerous volcano in the USA.

Most active volcano

The most active volcano on Earth is Kilauea in Hawaii. It has been spewing lava non-stop since 1983. The name Kilauea actually means "spewing!" You could pave a road around the world three times with all the lava that has erupted from it.

NATURAL WONDERS

Largest desert

The world's largest desert isn't covered in sand, it's covered in ice! Antarctica is called a desert because it gets very little rain. It covers more than 8.6 million square miles in the winter, when there's lots of ice.

Longest-lasting rainbow

Everyone loves a rainbow, but they vanish all too soon. The folks living in Wetherby, in West Yorkshire, England, had a special treat on March 14, 1994. A rainbow appeared after a rain shower and stayed in the sky for a record-breaking 6 hours! I wonder if they found a pot of gold at the end of it?

Coldest village

The coldest village you could live in is Oymyakon in Siberia, Russia, where the temperature has been known to fall to -89.9°F. That's the coldest temperature ever recorded outside Antarctica!

Largest island

The world's largest island is Greenland, which is ruled by Denmark. It is 836,330 square miles in size and more than 80 percent is covered in ice. Greenland isn't green at all!

Cavers said exploring the Krubera Cave was like scaling an upside-down Mount Everest

Deepest cave

The deepest cave in the world goes down 7,188 feet into the Earth. It is the Krubera Cave, which is found near the Black Sea, in Georgia, Eurasia. It's probably even deeper, but so far, that's as deep as cavers have managed to descend!

MAN-MADE MARVELS

Tallest man-made structure

The tallest man-made structure on the planet is the Burj Khalifa building in Dubai, which is in the United Arab Emirates. At 2,717 feet, this skyscraper is 1,267 feet taller than America's tallest building, the Willis Tower in Chicago, Illinois. The Burj Khalifa was opened in 2010 and cost $1.5 billion.

The Burj Khalifa has more than 160 stories and an elevator with the longest travel distance in the world.

Largest passenger ship

Like a massive floating town, the world's largest passenger ship is the 225,282-ton *Allure of the Seas*. This mammoth liner is 1,181 feet long, has 16 decks, carries 6,400 passengers, and even has its own ice rink.

World's highest bridge

The world's highest bridge is the Si Du River Bridge in Hubei, China. It is 1,627 feet above ground and spans 2,950 feet between mountain ranges. Don't look down!

Longest runway

The longest airport runway in the world stretches 18,045 feet and can be found at Qamdo Bangda Airport in Tibet, China. It is also the highest airport in the world, scraping the clouds at 14,219 feet.

DID YOU KNOW? DID YOU KNOW? DID YOU KNOW? DID YOU KNOW? DID YOU KNOW? DID YOU KNOW?

The first computer mouse was made by an American, Douglas Engelbart, in 1964. He called it a mouse because its wire looked like a mouse's tail.

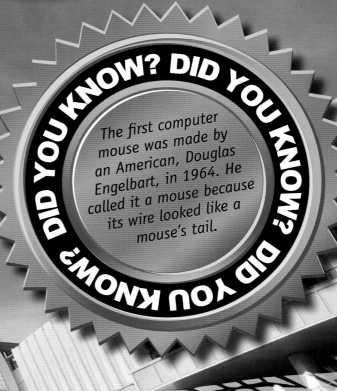

Biggest stadium

America's biggest football stadium is the Michigan Stadium in Ann Arbor, which can hold 111,000 people, including staff and bands. Affectionately known as The Big House, it is home to the Michigan Wolverines.

MAN-MADE MARVELS

Longest man-made structure

The Great Wall of China is the longest man-made structure in the world. The 2,150 mile-long wall was originally built to protect the Chinese Empire from **invasion** in the 7th century **B.C.E.**

Most widely used

The World Wide Web, more commonly known as the Internet, was the idea of British computer scientist Tim Berners-Lee in 1990. He says he first got into computers because he enjoyed studying math at school!

Despite the **myth**, U.S. Apollo astronauts say the Great Wall cannot be seen from space.

RECORD BREAKER

The fastest-selling electronic device of all time is the Apple iPad. When it went on sale in 2010, 3 million iPads were sold in the first 80 days alone!

Most distant man-made object

The man-made object that has traveled the farthest from Earth is NASA's Voyager 1 space probe, which was launched in 1997. It has traveled more than 11 billion miles and is still spinning through space!

Largest man-made islands

The largest man-made islands are made of totora reeds and float on Lake Titicaca in Peru and Bolivia. There are 42 islands and hundreds of people from the Uros tribe live on them. They constantly have to repair the islands, as the reeds rot quickly in the water!

Oldest man-made structure

The oldest wooden man-made structure in the world is the Hōryū-ji Temple in Ikaruga, Nara Prefecture, Japan. The name means "Temple of the Flourishing Law." It was built in 607 CE by Prince Shōtoku.

MAN-MADE MARVELS

Most epic structure

One of the most **epic** structures ever built is the Great Pyramid at Giza in Egypt. It was the tomb of Pharaoh Khufu, who was King of Egypt nearly 4,500 years ago. It was 481 feet 3 inches tall, took 20 years to build using 2.3 million huge stone blocks, and was the world's tallest building for 3,800 years!

Largest palace

The largest palace ever built is the home of His Majesty the Sultan of Brunei, in Southeast Asia. It cost $422 million and covers 2,152,780 square feet. That's roughly as big as 40 football fields laid side by side!

The Great Pyramid is the only one of the Seven Wonders of the Ancient World that is still standing.

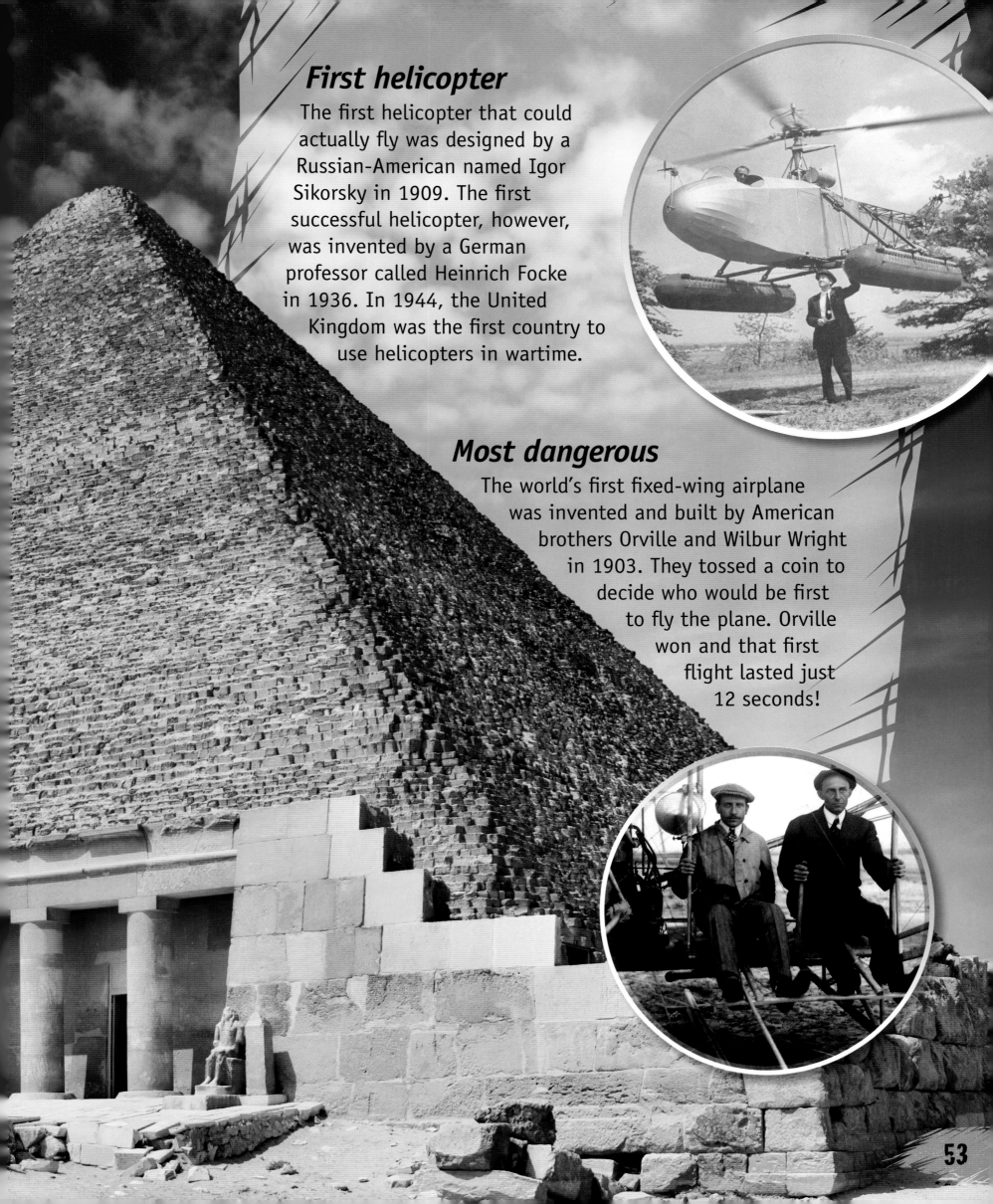

First helicopter

The first helicopter that could actually fly was designed by a Russian-American named Igor Sikorsky in 1909. The first successful helicopter, however, was invented by a German professor called Heinrich Focke in 1936. In 1944, the United Kingdom was the first country to use helicopters in wartime.

Most dangerous

The world's first fixed-wing airplane was invented and built by American brothers Orville and Wilbur Wright in 1903. They tossed a coin to decide who would be first to fly the plane. Orville won and that first flight lasted just 12 seconds!

MAN-MADE MARVELS

By 1918, half of the cars in the USA were Model-T Fords.

First affordable car

The world's first affordable ride was produced by Henry Ford in Detroit, Michigan, in 1908. It was called the Model-T Ford and nicknamed "Tin Lizzie." This was the car that eventually made driving popular. The first one cost $850, equal to about $21,987 today!

First gasoline car

The earliest American car to run on gasoline was built by brothers Charles and Frank Duryea, of Springfield, Massachusetts, in 1893. You can see it at the Smithsonian Institution in Washington, D.C.

RECORD BREAKER

The world's longest limousine stretches 100 feet and has 26 wheels! It is owned by Jay Ohrberg of Burbank, California.

First automobile

Karl Benz, a German designer, invented the first automobile in 1886. His wife, Bertha, was the world's first long-distance car driver. She drove 6 miles in 1888. That was a very long trip in those days!

First robotic car

Designers expect the world's first robotic car (one that doesn't need a driver) to be on our roads by 2020. It would be able to sense everything around it and navigate to a destination on its own. How cool is that?

First self-propelled road vehicle

The first self-propelled road vehicle was built by a French inventor called Nicolas-Joseph Cugnot in 1769. It was a three-wheeler powered by steam.

EXCEPTIONAL COUNTRIES

Longest coral reef

Australia's Great Barrier Reef is the longest natural coral reef in the world. It stretches for 1,260 miles and is home to whales, dolphins, porpoises, turtles, and even sea snakes. The reef is so large it can be seen from space!

The coldest temperature ever recorded was -128.6°F at Vostok Research Station, Antarctica, on July 21, 1983. Perfect igloo weather!

DID YOU KNOW? DID YOU KNOW? DID YOU KNOW? DID YOU KNOW?

Hottest temperature

The hottest temperature ever recorded was a sweltering 136°F in El Azizia, in Libya, northern Africa, on September 13, 1922. Sunscreen wouldn't have helped that day! The highest summer temperature ever recorded in the USA was in Death Valley, California, where it reached 134°F on July 10, 1913. Death Valley is now mainly **scorched** desert, but around 1 million years ago it was a huge inland sea!

Steepest road

The steepest road on Earth travels up the Haleakala volcano in Maui, Hawaii. The volcano is 10,023 feet high. The ascent is so high you can get altitude sickness!

Smallest country

The world's smallest country is Vatican City State in Rome, Italy. It covers just 0.2 square miles and only around 800 people live there, including the Pope of the Catholic Church. The country is so small there are no street names!

About 350 types of coral live on the Great Barrier Reef.

EXCEPTIONAL COUNTRIES

Largest country

Russia is the largest country in the world, covering 6,601,668 square miles. It has 83 federal subjects, which are like states. The USA is the fourth largest country and has 50 states.

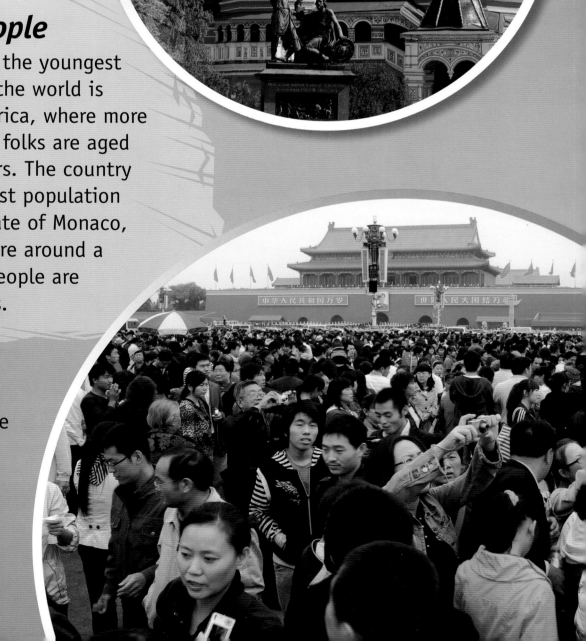

Youngest people

The country with the youngest **population** in the world is Uganda, in Africa, where more than half the folks are aged under 15 years. The country with the oldest population is the tiny state of Monaco, in Europe, where around a quarter of the people are aged over 65 years.

Largest population

The country in the world with the most people is China. A mind-boggling 1,339,190,000 people live there. The US has around 310,000,000 people, so you can see the huge difference!

Most populous U.S. city

The U.S. city that has the most people is New York. There are almost 20 million people living and working there. Did you know that New York was America's capital city for one year (1789 to 1790)?

The Statue of Liberty in New York Harbor was a gift from the people of France.

Most densely populated city

The most densely populated city in the world is Tokyo, Japan. Nearly 33 million people live there and sometimes the trains get so crowded that the railway staff are paid to shove them all inside the carriages!

RECORD BREAKER

There are around 7 billion people living on our planet. That's the largest number of people that have ever lived on Earth at the same time!

EXCEPTIONAL COUNTRIES

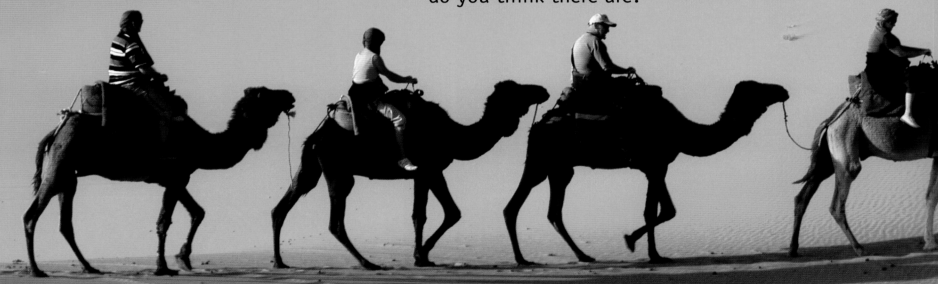

Largest sandy desert

The world's largest sandy desert is the Sahara, North Africa, which covers over 3.5 million square miles. How many grains of sand do you think there are?

Rarest language

The least-spoken language on the planet is Yaghan. This was the language of the people of Tierra del Fuego, in South America. Now only one full-blooded Yaghan remains. Her name is Cristina Calderón and she is around 85 years old.

Most densely populated country

Monaco, in Europe, is the most densely populated country in the world. That means it has the highest number of people living in the smallest space. Some 46,436 people live in every square mile!

RECORD BREAKER

Chinese Mandarin is spoken by 1 billion people, making it the most spoken language in the world.

Most twisters

Most people think the USA has more tornado twisters than any other country in the world. It might surprise you to know that the Netherlands has more! That country experiences one twister for every 769 square miles of land.

Highest mountain

The highest mountain on Earth is Mount Everest in the Himalayas, between China and Nepal, which rises to 29,029 feet. But the tallest mountain overall is Mauna Kea in Hawaii, USA. How come? Although you can only see 13,796 feet of Mauna Kea above ground, there's another 19,684 feet underwater, making it 33,480 feet tall!

EXCEPTIONAL COUNTRIES

Free space

No country or person can own the Moon or any of the planets, even if they landed there first. The Outer Space Treaty of 1967 doesn't allow anyone on Earth to own anything in space, except the rockets and satellites they launch there. Sounds fair!

Most remote

The most remote inhabited island on the planet is Tristan da Cunha in the southern Atlantic. This island is the farthest away from anywhere else on Earth. There are only around 250 people living there and they are all related, so they share just seven surnames!

Smallest island

The smallest island in the world is Bishop Rock, southwest of the United Kingdom. It only has space for a lighthouse on it!

There's a helipad on top of the remote Bishop Rock lighthouse.

DID YOU KNOW? DID YOU KNOW? DID YOU KNOW? DID YOU KNOW?

The United Kingdom is the only island in the world that is connected to a continent through a tunnel under the sea. It's called The Chunnel and it connects England to France.

Largest continent

The world's largest **continent** is Asia, which covers 17,139,445 square miles. Africa is the second largest, covering 11,668,599 square miles of land. North America is the third largest, with land covering 9,361,791 square miles.

Farthest inland location

The piece of land that is the farthest from any sea is the Dzungarian Basin in China. It is 1,645 miles from the coast and is mainly desert. In 2006, U.S. scientists dug up the world's oldest **tyrannosaur** fossil in the Dzungarian Basin. It was 160 million years old!

AMAZING SPACE

A black hole is filled with a lot of material crammed into an extremely small space.

Densest object in the universe

The densest thing in the whole universe is a black hole in space. **Gravity** is so strong there that not even light can escape from it. Black holes are formed when a huge star dies. The biggest black holes are called "supermassives."

Most distant visible object

The most distant object in the universe that can be seen through NASA's powerful Hubble Space Telescope is GRB 090429B. That's the label scientists have put on a pale red dot they think is a **gamma-ray** burst that is 13.2 billion light years away from Earth!

Biggest explosion

The "Big Bang" was the biggest explosion that ever took place in space. It happened 13.7 billion years ago and that's when some people think the universe and all the planets were created. Nobody knows what there was before the Big Bang, because that's when time (as we know it) began!

Fastest space objects

The fastest objects spinning through space are bubbles of superheated **plasma** that were spat out by black holes. Some have been recorded moving at 99.99% of the speed of light.

Farthest planet

The farthest planet from the Sun in our solar system is Neptune. It is 2.8 billion miles away and it has the fastest winds in the solar system. Gusts blow across its surface at 1,500 miles per hour. Hang on to your space helmet!

AMAZING SPACE

Largest planet

The largest planet in our solar system is the mighty Jupiter. Earth could fit inside Jupiter more than 1,300 times! At its equator (around the middle), it measures 88,846 miles across. The giant red spot that can be seen on its surface is a terrible storm that has been raging for 300 years! Jupiter also has the shortest day. One day only lasts 9 hours 55 minutes and 29.69 seconds!

Jupiter has the strongest magnetic field in the solar system.

Smoothest moon

The smoothest surface in the solar system belongs to Europa, which is one of Jupiter's moons. Europa is almost completely covered in ice. Some scientists believe that **extraterrestrial** life could exist in the water under Europa's ice. E.T. swim home?

DID YOU KNOW? DID YOU KNOW? DID YOU KNOW? DID YOU KNOW?

The first **asteroid** to crash to Earth from space happened 3.47 billion years ago! In 2002, U.S. scientists found bits of it scattered as far apart as Australia and South Africa.

Coldest place in space

The coldest place in space is the Boomerang Nebula, which is a cloud of dust and gas. It is 5,000 light years from Earth and the temperature there gets as low as -457.6°F. Brrr!

Most craters

The object with the most craters in the solar system is Callisto, one of Jupiter's moons. It also has the oldest surface. Nothing has changed there for more than 4 billion years.

Smelliest moon?

The moon with the most active volcanoes in the solar system is Io, another of Jupiter's many moons. Its surface is covered in sulfur, which spouts from the volcanoes. Sulfur smells like rotten eggs, so Io must be one smelly moon!

RECORD-BREAKING KIDS

Biggest baby

The world's biggest baby was born in Italy in 1955. The not-so-little boy weighed 22 pounds 8 ounces. The average weight for a newborn baby in the USA is 7½ pounds. His mom must have been pretty tired carrying him around!

Strongest boy

A five-year-old boy put adult bodybuilders to shame when he managed to perform 20 air push-ups live on TV in Romania, in Central Europe. Guiliano Stroe broke the previous world record of 12 air push-ups, which was set by a grown-up. Guiliano is now officially "The World's Strongest Boy."

RECORD BREAKER

Tara Kristen Lipinski of the USA was the youngest person to win the Olympic gold medal in figure skating. She was just 14 when she competed in the 1998 Winter Olympics in Nagano, Japan.

Most digits

A baby in India was born with 34 fingers and toes. Akshat Saxena had seven fingers on each hand and ten toes on each foot. The two-year-old boy has since had a successful operation to remove some of his extra digits.

First human cannonball

The first ever human cannonball was a 14-year-old circus performer named "Zazel," who was fired 30 feet from a spring-loaded cannon in London, England, in 1877. Zazel's real name was Rossa Matilda Richter. She worked with the famous American showman P.T. Barnum, but she had to retire after hurting her back in a fall.

Biggest sleepover

The world's biggest sleepover took place across the United Kingdom, when more than 40,000 kids gave up their beds and slept outdoors to raise cash for a children's charity. As well as raising thousands of dollars, the sleepover kids won themselves a place in the record books.

TERRIFIC TOYS

First teddy

The first stuffed toy bear with movable arms and legs was made by the Steiff Company in Germany, Europe, in 1902. Americans made the bear popular and it was renamed the "Teddy bear" after President Theodore "Teddy" Roosevelt in 1906.

Steiff bears were given swivel joints to make them easier to cuddle!

Oldest doll's head

The world's oldest doll's head was dug up in 2004 on the Italian island of Pantelleria. The 4,000-year-old stone head had a carved face and curly hair. Its body was probably made of wood or cloth but sadly did not survive being buried in mud.

Longest toy train track

The world's longest toy train track was laid out in Yamanashi, Japan, in 2011. It stretched 7,288 feet and took 10,575 pieces of plastic track to complete. Kids and parents from all over Japan took part in building it.

Largest jigsaw

If you enjoy jigsaw puzzles, you would love the 32,256-piece jigsaw produced by Ravensburger AG in Germany. It measures 17 feet by 6 feet, weighs 42 pounds, and when completed it shows 32 paintings by the pop artist Keith Haring. It's so heavy its box comes with wheels!

DID YOU KNOW? DID YOU KNOW? DID YOU KNOW? DID YOU KNOW? DID YOU KNOW?

According to the National Toy Hall of Fame, the world's oldest toy was probably... a stick!

Biggest game of Monopoly

The toy company Hasbro organized the world's biggest game of Monopoly in 2008, when 2,918 people in 21 countries took part in an online game. Monopoly is the most popular board game ever. It is sold in 81 countries and has been translated into 27 languages!

TERRIFIC TOYS

First collectible doll

The first collectible doll based on a **licensed** character was Scarlett O'Hara, from the movie *Gone with the Wind*. It was made by American doll maker Madame Alexander in 1937.

RECORD BREAKER

An Australian yo-yo champion named Ben McPhee broke the record when he managed to get 16 yo-yos spinning at one time. Two were hung from his ears and two were hung from his mouth!

Most valuable toy pistols

The most valuable and rare pair of toy pistols is a set of "Whistling Bird" pistols made in Switzerland, in 1820. They are the only surviving pair and are worth $5.8 million today. When you press the jeweled pistol's trigger, a tiny, feathered bird pops out of the barrel, flaps its wings, and starts to sing!

Longest ramp jump

The longest ramp jump by a remote-control car was 112 feet 7.5 inches. This mega jump was achieved in 2011 by Robert Kinch, from Oil City, Pennsylvania, with his Traxxas E-REVO 1/10 scale electric truck.

Most valuable Star Wars figure

The most valuable Star Wars action figure is the "Telescoping Lightsaber" Darth Vader, first sold in 1978. Only a few hundred of these were ever made, because the lightsaber kept breaking. This means that collectors are willing to pay up to $6,000 for one of these small plastic figures. Check out your dad's old toy chest!

It took 3 actors to portray Darth Vader in the movies: David Prowse (body), Sebastian Shaw (face), and James Earl Jones (voice)!

Rarest PEZ dispenser

The world's rarest PEZ dispenser is the 1982 World Fair Astronaut B PEZ Dispenser. Only two were ever made and one was **auctioned** on the Internet for $32,205!

CURIOUS COLLECTIONS

Most rubber ducks

Would you like to take a bath with 5,249 rubber ducks? A university professor named Charlotte Lee can! She has been collecting rubber ducks since 1996 and has the biggest collection in the world. She keeps them in a special room at her home in Seattle, Washington.

Most masks

The world's largest collection of masks belongs to Gerold Weschenmoser of Germany. He has gathered 5,385 different masks since 1957. Does this make him the ultimate master of disguise?

Largest Barbie collection

"There's nothing I don't know about Barbie," says Bettina Dorfmann of Dusseldorf, Germany. Since she has collected 6,025 of the fashion dolls, she is probably correct! Her collection is worth a staggering $162,000, but she says she won't stop collecting Barbies until she reaches 10,000.

Biggest ball of wrap

The world record for rolling the biggest ball of plastic wrap is held by 12-year-old Josh Lonsway of Bay City, Michigan. His giant roll of plastic measures 138 inches in diameter, weighs 282 pounds, and took 8 months to complete. That's **sheer** madness!

RECORD BREAKER

Nabil Karam from Lebanon, in the Middle East, owns the world's largest collection of model cars. He has a car-tastic 22,222 miniature four-wheelers.

Largest shoe collection

The world's largest collection of shoes, old and new, is owned by the Northampton Museum and Art Gallery in England. They have 12,000 pairs on display, including a pair worn by Queen Victoria on her wedding day in 1840, and a **tribal** shoe made from a crocodile's foot that's complete with claws. That's shoe business!

CURIOUS COLLECTIONS

Donald devotee

The person with the most Donald Duck **memorabilia** is Mary Brooks of the USA, who has collected 1,411 different objects related to the Disney cartoon character. Funnily enough, her husband is named Donald and his nickname at school was "Duck!"

Donald Duck was created in 1934.

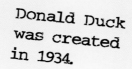

Condiment collection

A retired truck driver named LaVerne Tish, of Missouri, has collected 6,971 pairs of salt and pepper shakers since 1984. Doesn't he know that too much salt is bad for you?

Largest collection of teddy bears

The biggest collection of teddy bears belongs to Jackie Miley of Hill City, South Dakota, who has **amassed** 7,106 different bears since 2002. She has so many that they now live in a separate house across the street from her, called "Teddy Bear Town."

Phone fan

When the telephone rings in Rita Zimmermann's house in Switzerland, she must have a hard time figuring out which one to pick up. She collected 771 telephones between 1990 and 2010 but has since "hung up" on her record-breaking hobby.

DID YOU KNOW? DID YOU KNOW? DID YOU KNOW? DID YOU KNOW?

The biggest private collection of comic books belongs to Brett Chilman of Henley Brook, Australia. Known as "The Comic Book Guy," he has collected more than 68,000 comics in 30 years.

Most Smurfs memorabilia

An Englishman holds the world record for the biggest collection of Smurfs memorabilia. Steve Ward, from Nottingham, UK, began collecting the little blue characters when he was young. He now has more than 1,070 Smurfs, the most valuable of which is a Gloria Milk Smurf, worth $1,291!

CURIOUS COLLECTIONS

The Beatles were formed in Liverpool, UK, in 1960.

Navel-gazer

One of the grossest collections of all time has to be that of Graham Barker from Perth, Australia. The 47-year-old librarian collects his own belly button lint! He has saved 0.75 ounces of navel fluff in carefully-labeled glass jars since 1984, which is a world record. Ewww!

Biggest Beatles collection

A fan of the world's biggest-selling rock group, The Beatles, broke records of his own when he opened a Beatles Museum in Buenos Aires, Argentina. Rodolfo Vazquez has collected 8,500 pieces of Beatles-related memorabilia, which he intends to put on display.

Clown collector

Clowns give some people nightmares, while others just love their fun antics. A 62 year-old German woman named Orty Kastaun must belong to the second group, because she has collected 2,053 different model clowns. Trick or treat..?

Biggest chocoholic

The world's biggest chocolate bar fan is Bob Brown of Indianapolis, Indiana. He has 770 different chocolate bars in his collection. It must be very tempting to indulge in a midnight feast!

Record jewelry sale

Hollywood movie star Elizabeth Taylor collected fabulous pieces of jewelry throughout her life. After she died in 2011, her collection was auctioned at Christie's in New York and sold for a record-breaking $116 million. The star of the show was a necklace with a 16th century pearl. It sold for a dazzling $11.8 million!

EXTRAORDINARILY EXPENSIVE

Most expensive car

The most expensive car in the world is the Bugatti Veyron Supersport, which costs a cool $2.6 million. It is also the fastest car on the road, with a teeth-rattling top speed of 267 miles per hour!

DID YOU KNOW? DID YOU KNOW? DID YOU KNOW? DID YOU KNOW? DID YOU KNOW?

The $250 million Hope Diamond is the most precious stone in the world. It is a 45.52-**carat**, deep blue stone and is now in the Smithsonian Natural History Museum in Washington, D.C.

Most expensive watch

Swiss watchmaker Hublot produced the world's most expensive watch in 2012. Carrying a price tag of $5 million, the watch has 1,292 diamonds inlaid on a white gold bracelet. Now we know what people mean when they say, "Time is money!"

Most expensive shoes

To mark the 50th anniversary of the popular movie *The Wizard of Oz*, New York jeweler Harry Winston created a real pair of ruby slippers. The shoes cost $3 million and are encrusted in 4,600 rubies and diamonds. Oh my!

One of the original four pairs of slippers worn in the 1939 movie is in the Smithsonian Museum.

Most expensive yacht

What's 98 feet long, carries 220,000 pounds of gold and platinum, and has a statue made from the bone of a genuine T-rex dinosaur? The answer is the world's most expensive yacht! Costing $4.5 billion, the gold-plated *History Supreme* was built in Malaysia, in Southeast Asia, for a mystery businessman.

EXTRAORDINARILY EXPENSIVE

Most expensive coffee

The world's most expensive coffee is processed from cat droppings! Civet coffee costs $80 a cup and is brewed in Indonesia. Coffee cherries are devoured by civet cats and pass through their digestive systems. The beans are then harvested from the cat's poop. Eww!

DID YOU KNOW? DID YOU KNOW? DID YOU KNOW? DID YOU KNOW?

Apple Inc. has produced a diamond-covered version of the iPhone 4S. It is the most expensive cell phone in the world—worth $9.4 million!

Most expensive home

With an incredible 27 stories, the world's most expensive family home is practically a skyscraper! Worth $2 billion, it has three helipads, six car parks, and floating gardens. The house is owned by billionaire Mukesh Ambani and is located in Mumbai, India.

Most expensive sushi

The world's most expensive **sushi** costs $1,975.15 for just five pieces! Filipino chef Angelito Araneta Jr. serves 0.2-carat African diamonds on top of **edible** gold leaf seaweed at his restaurant in Manila. That's expensive taste!

Most expensive bathroom

The world's most expensive bathroom, made entirely of 24-carat gold, is in Hong Kong, China. The lavatory is not for sale, but its owners say they may melt it down when the price of gold reaches $1,000 per ounce, leaving them "flush" with $32 million.

Most expensive dog

A Red Tibetan Mastiff dog is the most expensive dog on the planet. The dog, called "Hong Dong" (Chinese for "Big Splash"), was sold for $1 million in China in 2011. Although still a puppy, it was 3 feet tall and weighed 180 pounds. Tibetan Mastiffs were bred as guard dogs, but at that price it's the dog that needs a guard!

MARVELOUS MOVIES

Most successful film

The most successful animated film in history is Disney Pixar's *Toy Story 3*, which broke the box office record in 2010. Go Woody!

Most awards

The 1959 film *Ben Hur*, starring Charlton Heston, was the first movie ever to win 11 Academy Awards (also known as the Oscars). *Ben Hur* held the record for 38 years, before the movie *Titanic* matched it in 1997. The third film to win 11 Oscars was *The Lord of the Rings: The Return of the King* in 2003.

The Oscar statuette depicts a knight standing on a reel of film.

Most nominated

Katharine Hepburn won the most Academy Awards during her long career. She collected a record-breaking four Oscars. The actor who has been nominated for an Oscar the most times is Meryl Streep. She has been nominated 17 times and has won three Oscars so far.

Highest earning

The film that earned the most dollars at the box office worldwide was *Avatar*, in 2009. Made by Canadian producer and director James Cameron, it is the most successful film of all time. He also made *Titanic* (1997), which was the previous highest-grossing film.

DID YOU KNOW? DID YOU KNOW? DID YOU KNOW? DID YOU KNOW? DID YOU KNOW?

The longest Oscar acceptance speech was given by British actress Greer Garson in 1942. She won Best Actress for Mrs. Miniver (1942) and thanked everyone she knew for five minutes and 30 seconds!

Most successful actor

The most successful actor in history, based on how much money his films have earned, is Samuel L. Jackson. His movies have made a record breaking $8.5 billion worldwide! So far he has starred in more than 70 movies.

85

MARVELOUS MOVIES

First robot

The first American movie to feature a robot (or mechanical man) was *The Mechanical Statue and the Ingenious Servant* in 1907.

Janet Leigh's character in *Psycho* flushed the toilet shortly before being stabbed. However, the shower was the real bathroom star of this movie.

First flush

The first toilet ever flushed in a movie was seen (and heard) in director Alfred Hitchcock's 1960 film *Psycho*, starring U.S. actor Anthony Perkins. It was considered quite scandalous at the time!

Most expensive movie

The most expensive movie ever made is Disney's *Pirates of the Caribbean: At World's End*. It cost $300,000,000 to film, but the **franchise** has so far earned more than $2.6 billion worldwide, so it was a good investment!

Largest movie tank

The 17-million-gallon seawater tank built for the sinking scene in the movie *Titanic* (1997) is the largest movie tank in the world and the biggest ever made for a movie. It looked pretty convincing, too!

Longest film

The longest movie ever made is *The Burning of the Red Lotus Temple*. It lasts a record-breaking 27 hours! It has never been shown in one straight sitting, but was cut into 18 different feature movies, shown from 1928 to 1931. Do you think you could sit in a movie theater for 27 hours straight? That would be a world record!

FOOD, GLORIOUS FOOD

Largest apple

The largest apple was a 4-pound, 1-ounce whopper grown by Japanese farmer Chisato Iwasaki, in Hirosaki City, Japan, in 2005. Did you know a quarter of an apple's **volume** is air? That's why apples float!

DID YOU KNOW? DID YOU KNOW? DID YOU KNOW? DID YOU KNOW?

Strawberries are the only fruit with seeds on the outside of their skin. There are about 200 seeds on each strawberry!

Heaviest carrot

The heaviest carrot in the world weighed 18 pounds 13 ounces and belonged to John Evans of Alaska. Did you know that creamed carrots were one of the last dishes served on the doomed *Titanic*?

Heaviest head of garlic

The heaviest head of garlic was grown by Robert Kirkpatrick in the awesomely named Eureka, California, in 1985. It weighed 2 pounds 10 ounces and was stinky enough to keep a whole coven of vampires away!

Largest peach

Paul Friday of Coloma, Michigan, holds the world record for growing the largest peach. Paul's peach tipped the scales at 25.6 ounces in 2002. He has since grown a peach that weighed 4.9 ounces more.

The average pumpkin weighs between 10 and 20 pounds.

Largest pumpkin

The world's largest pumpkin was grown in Quebec, Canada, by Jim Bryson and his daughter, Kelsey, in 2011. It weighed a remarkable 1,818.5 pounds!

FOOD, GLORIOUS FOOD

Oldest recipe

The oldest written recipe was discovered carved into clay tablets by archeologists digging in ancient Mesopotamia (now part of Iraq). The recipe is 4,000 years old. Is it from some ancient king's **extravagant** banquet? No...it's a recipe for beer!

Cuneiform script is one of the earliest forms of writing.

Highest pancake toss

The world's highest pancake toss is 31 feet. The pancake was flipped and caught by record breaker Mike Cuzzacrea at the Walden Galleria in Cheektowaga, New York, on November 24, 2010.

Biggest omelet

If you like eggs, you'd have enjoyed the 9,702.5-pound omelet served at the Cepa shopping mall in Ankara, Turkey, on October 8, 2010. Eighty chefs cracked 110,000 eggs into a 33-foot skillet containing 95 gallons of oil.

Most expensive treat

Caviar (basically, fish eggs) is one of the world's most expensive treats. The costliest caviar is an Iranian beluga called "Almas." It is a pale amber color and comes from 100-year-old sturgeon fish. Just 3.9 pounds of the caviar costs $48,750!

RECORD BREAKER

The fastest time for shelling a boiled egg is 18.95 seconds. The record was set by Alastair Galpin of Auckland, New Zealand, in 2009. Care to try to break it?

Largest hamburger

The largest hamburger you can buy in a restaurant is a 300-pound, 4-ounce meat feast! It is served at the Phoenix Seagaia Resort in Miyazaki, Japan, for a modest $1,780. Its weight is the **equivalent** of 796 quarterpounders!

ASTOUNDING ADVENTURES

South Pole speed record

The fastest solo journey to the frozen South Pole was completed on skis in 24 days, 1 hour, and 13 minutes by Christian Eide of Norway in 2011. That will be a hard record to beat!

DID YOU KNOW? DID YOU KNOW? DID YOU KNOW? DID YOU KNOW? DID YOU KNOW?

A 104-year-old from Scotland is the oldest person ever to paraglide. Wheelchair user Peggy McAlpine leaped from a 2,400-foot (731.5-m) mountain for her record breaking flight across Cyprus in 2012.

Record run

From San Francisco on the west coast to New York City on the east coast is 3,100 miles. That was the distance run by American Frank Giannino Jr. in a record-breaking time of 46 days, 8 hours, and 36 minutes in 1980. He must have had blisters on his blisters!

More than 3,000 people have successfully climbed Everest since Hillary and Tensing's first ascent.

First Everest ascent

Climbing Mount Everest, the world's highest mountain at 29,029 feet, is the dream of many adventurers. The first men to reach the top were New Zealand climber Edmund Hillary and his Nepalese Sherpa, Tensing Norgay, in May 1953.

Longest motorcycle trip

The farthest motorcycle journey was by Emilio Scotto from Argentina on his Honda Gold Wing. Between 1985 and 1995 he traveled 457,000 miles, visited 214 countries, learned five languages, met cannibals, and got married in India. That's some road trip!

ASTOUNDING ADVENTURES

Longest walk

The first man who claimed to have walked 55,000 miles right around the planet was an American named George Matthew Schilling. He set off from New York in 1897 and got home in 1904!

First around-the-world balloon flight

The first around-the-world hot air balloon flight lasted 19 days, 21 hours, and 47 minutes and covered 25,361 miles. The epic trip was made in 1999 by Brian Jones of the UK and Bertrand Piccard of Switzerland in a balloon named *Breitling Orbiter 3*.

Longest time at sea

A British rower Roz Savage was the first woman to row single-handedly across both the Atlantic and Pacific Oceans. She spent nearly 250 days at sea and during that time her boat capsized, her oars were smashed by waves, and she lost her stove, **navigation** instruments, and even her music player.

Youngest solo flier

The youngest person to fly solo around the world in a light airplane was 23-year-old Barrington Antonio Irving Jr, from Kingston, Jamaica. He flew 30,000 miles through **monsoon** rains, snow, and storms in a Cessna 400 in 2007.

RECORD BREAKER

Alex Honnold from Sacramento, climbed 3,000 feet to the summit of El Capitan, a steep rock in Yosemite National Park, California, three times in 24 hours. He broke the record for the fastest number of climbs in a row.

Longest hang-glider flight

The longest flight by a hang glider, powered only by the wind, was 435.33 miles. The nail-biting trip was made by Manfred Ruhmer of Austria, who glided from Zapata County to Lamesa in Texas, in 2001.

More hang-gliding records have been set from Zapata, Texas, than from any other location.

DON'T TRY THIS AT HOME

Most dangerous sky sport

The most dangerous sky sport is banzai skydiving. It involves flying to 10,000 feet, throwing your parachute out the airplane, waiting two seconds, and jumping out after it. The aim is to catch it, put it on, and pull the ripcord before you hit the ground. Yikes!

DID YOU KNOW? DID YOU KNOW? DID YOU KNOW? DID YOU KNOW?

Tyler Bradt, from Montana, steered his kayak off the Palouse Falls in Washington State and plummeted 186 feet into the water below. The 22-year-old survived with nothing worse than a sprained wrist.

Record smasher

A man named Davide Cenciarelli from Italy, managed to smash 70 watermelons in 60 seconds using just his fist. That had to hurt!

Car carrying record

Weightlifter Mark Anglesea lifted an 837-pound car and carried it a record breaking 1,337 feet in Rotherham, England. Mark also holds the record for lifting a 1,175-pound Mini Metro car 580 times in one hour in 1998! That is one strong man.

The extreme sport of banzai skydiving started in Japan.

Most bungee jumps

The record number of bungee jumps in 60 minutes was by James Field of London, UK. He managed 42 using a cord measuring 19 feet 8 inches. Bet he felt sick to his stomach by the end of it!

Most kicks to head

A Swiss man kicked himself in the head 110 times in one minute in Lausanne, Switzerland, in 2010. That's one way to guarantee a headache!

DON'T TRY THIS AT HOME

RECORD BREAKER

Wim Hof from the Netherlands holds 18 world records, including one for being buried in ice for 1 hour, 52 minutes, and 42 seconds in 2011.

Fastest onion peeler

Canadian Bob Blumer cried his way to a world record when he peeled 31 onions weighing 50 pounds in 2 minutes 39 seconds. Pass that man a tissue.

Record breaking free dive

Not content with holding his breath for a record-breaking 20 minutes and 10 seconds underwater, free diver Stig Åvall Severinsen from Denmark did it in a tank full of sharks!

Heaviest house haul

Kevin Fast dragged a 79,145-pound house almost 40 feet in Ontario, Canada, on September 18, 2010. He should have called a moving company.

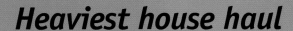
Apart from hauling a house, Kevin Fast has pulled trucks, and even a plane.

Most coconuts smashed

Martial arts fan Muhamed Kahrimanovic, from Germany, smashed 111 coconuts using just his hands and entered the record books in 2011. His hands must have been the size of baseball mitts after that stunt!

Fastest escapologist

The world's fastest escapologist is American Jackson Rayne, who escaped from a straitjacket in 7.26 seconds in Las Vegas, Nevada, in 2009. That's faster than Houdini!

WEIRD AND AMAZING

DID YOU KNOW? DID YOU KNOW? DID YOU KNOW? DID YOU KNOW?

In 2003, American John Cassidy made 529 balloon animals in just one hour!

Most golf balls held

The record for holding the most golf balls in one hand belongs jointly to Canadian Guillaume Doyon and Rohit Timilsina of Nepal. Both men held 24 golf balls in one hand for 10 seconds. Sounds easy? Try it!

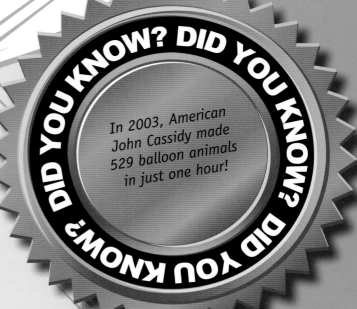

Michel Lotito cuts metal objects into bite–size pieces and eats a little each day.

Strangest diet

A Frenchman became the first person in the world to eat a whole airplane—metal, glass, rubber and all! Michel Lotito ate the Cessna 150 airplane between 1978 and 1980. He began eating **bizarre** things when he was just nine. Strangely, the only time he got sick was eating bananas and boiled eggs!

Longest-bearded lady

America has its own record breaking bearded lady! Vivian Wheeler from Illinois sports a beard that measures 10.9 inches. She's proud of it, too.

Longest fingernails

The longest fingernails on the planet belong to Christine Walton from Las Vegas, Nevada. She spent 18 years growing them until they reached an amazing 10 feet 2 inches. She can still eat with a knife and fork and put on her make-up without poking herself in the eye!

Heaviest onion

The world's heaviest onion weighs 18 pounds and was grown by Peter Glazebrook in the UK. You'd cry a lot of tears if you peeled that monster onion!

WEIRD AND AMAZING

Biggest chocolate chip cookie

The biggest chocolate chip cookie ever baked was 102 feet across and weighed 38,000 pounds. It was made by the Immaculate Baking Company of North Carolina in 2003. Got cavities?

Fastest furniture

The world's fastest piece of furniture can zoom along at 130 miles per hour! It is a Queen Anne dinner table, complete with tableware, cloth, and chairs, powered by a Reliant Scimitar Sabre car engine. It was built by **eccentric** English inventor Perry Watkins in 2010.

Longest eyebrows

The world's longest eyebrows belong to Leonard Traenkenschuh of Port Townsend, Washington, DC. His eyebrow hair is 3½ inches long. That's enough to make your eyes water!

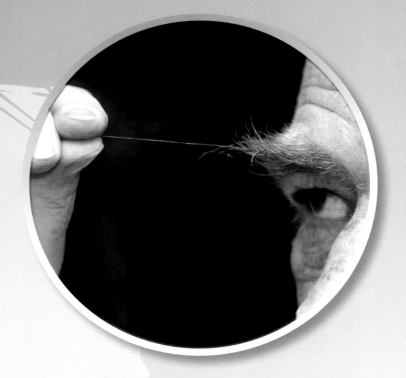

Biggest miser

The biggest **miser** in history was U.S. businesswoman Hetty Green. She made more than $100 million on **Wall Street** in the 19th century, but she never turned on the heating or hot water, and she wore the same black dress and undergarments until they fell apart! Ewww!

Stretchiest skin

The stretchiest human skin belongs to Garry Turner of Lincolnshire in England. He stretched his stomach skin to 6¼ inches on prime time TV in Los Angeles, California, in 1999. Is this the real Elastic Man?

RECORD BREAKER

Kim Goodman, from Chicago, Illinois, can pop her eyes out half an inch beyond her eye sockets. She discovered this talent when she was hit on the head by a hockey mask. It was an eye-popping experience!

Garry can cover his face with his super-stretchy neck skin.

WEIRD AND AMAZING

Theme park guests helped construct the Lego tower that soared above the park's entrance.

Tallest Lego tower

The world's tallest Lego tower was built at Legoland in Carlsbad, California, in 2005. It reached 92 feet 6 inches and took 12,000 people five days to complete, using 400,000 bricks. Phew!

Best balancing act

British man John Evans holds an awesome 34 world records for balancing very heavy objects on his head—including a 357-pound Mini Cooper car, a 20-foot vertical pole, and a kid's ATV! But not all at once...

Rattlesnake record

"The Texas Snake Man" certainly tries to live up to his nickname. Jackie Bibby holds four world records for doing weird and very dangerous things with rattlesnakes. He held eight live snakes in his mouth, shared a sleeping bag with 109 of the critters, sat in a bathtub with 87 rattlesnakes, and stuffed 10 of them in a sack in a record-breaking 17.11 seconds. Don't try these at home!

RECORD BREAKER

The world's oldest ever person was a lady named Jeanne Calment of France who died in 1997 when she was 122 years and 164 days.

Expert record-breaker

Ashrita Furman from Queens, New York, balanced a pool cue on his chin and managed to walk 5,472 feet 9 inches before it fell off. Ashrita is a bit of a record breaking expert. He currently holds 147 world records—including the record for having the most world records!

Biggest surfboard

The world's biggest surfboard is about the length of a school bus—40 feet—and can carry 47 adult surfers at one time. It was built by an Australian surfboard maker named Nev Hyman.

WEIRD AND AMAZING

Biggest bubble

The largest bubblegum bubble ever blown reached an impressive 20 inches in **diameter** before it burst. The record breaking pink bubble was blown by Chad Fell of Winston County, Alabama.

Longest paper plane flight

The world record distance for a paper airplane flight is 226 feet 10 inches. The paper arrow was thrown by former Berkley quarterback Joe Ayoob in an aircraft hangar in California in 2012. Think you can beat it?

Most T-shirts

The record for wearing the most T-shirts at the same time was set by a man in Croatia called Krunoslav Budiselic. He managed to pull 245 cotton T-shirts over his head before his head finally disappeared.

Most straws

A man from Switzerland holds the record for cramming the most drinking straws into his mouth. Marco Hort managed to squeeze 264 plastic straws into his mouth. Bet that made him thirsty!

Tallest motorcycle

The world's most mega motorcycle was built by Greg Dunham of Stockton, California. It measures 15 feet in height, 25 feet in length, and weighs over 6,500 pounds.

Greg Dunham built his huge bike on a bet!

RECORD BREAKER

The largest game of dodgeball ever played happened at the University of Alberta, in Canada, in 2011, when 2,012 competitors hurled balls at one another.

WEIRD AND AMAZING

Largest maze

The world's largest maze was created by a farmer in North Yorkshire, England. Tom Pearcy's Star Trek-inspired maze covers 32 acres, which is about the size of 15 football fields!

Rabbit record

In 2008, magicians Piero Ustignani and Walter Rolfo pulled a record 300 rabbits out of a hat during a 30-minute performance in Aosta, Italy. How did they get them all into one hat?

Longest mustache

Ram Singh Chauhan of India is the proud owner of the world's longest mustache! He has been growing his facial hair since 1982 and it now droops 14 feet from his upper lip!

Biggest stairclimb on a bike

The most steps ever climbed on a bicycle without falling off is 2,008. Three men share the record: Javier Zapata of Colombia, Zhang Jincheng of China, and Xavi Casas of Andorra. They bounced up all 88 floors of the Jin Mao Tower in Shanghai, China, on December 31, 2007.

Biggest bagel

The world's biggest bagel was shown at the New York State Fair in 2004. It was 20 inches thick, weighed 868 pounds and was 6 feet in diameter. It was so large it had to be moved by crane!

WEIRD AND AMAZING

Tallest teen

The world's tallest teenager is Brenden Adams of Ellensburg, Washington. Born in 1995, the amazing teen grew to 7 feet 4.5 inches. Doctors helped him to stop growing in 2008 because his height was affecting his health.

Biggest bunny

A rabbit named Darius is the world's biggest bunny. Darius, who lives with his owner Annette Edwards, in Worcestershire, England, is 4 feet 3 inches long, weighs 50 pounds and is still growing. That's hopping mad!

Largest game of Twister

The largest game of Twister ever played involved 400 people getting into a tangle on a game board measuring 4,717.8 square feet . It was played by students at University College Dublin, in Ireland, who **contorted** their way into the record books in March 2010.

Highest female kick

Movie stuntwoman Zara Phythian from Nottingham, England, holds the world record for the highest female martial arts kick. Known as "Lady Dragon," she leaped more than 7 feet to clinch the record in Beijing, China, in 2008. Nobody messes with this lady!

Zara Phythian began her martial arts training at the age of seven.

Biggest crowd in a bubble

The world record for enclosing the most people inside a single soap bubble is held by "Sam, Sam the Bubble Man." Sam Heath (that's his real name) used a huge wand to wave a 5-foot bubble around 19 boys and girls in Surrey, UK, in 2006.

WEIRD AND AMAZING

DID YOU KNOW? DID YOU KNOW? DID YOU KNOW? DID YOU KNOW?

The world's longest parade float stretched for 2,596.7 feet! It was part of the annual Lantern Festival in China. It was a paper and bamboo dragon connected by wooden planks.

Biggest litter of puppies

Tia, a Neopolitan mastiff, holds the world record for giving birth to the most puppies at one time. She delivered an astonishing 24 pups on November 29, 2004, at her home in Cambridgeshire, UK.

Biggest rubber band ball

The largest rubber band ball was created by Joel Waul of Lauderhill, Florida. The store worker made the 9,032-pound ball from 730,000 rubber bands in the driveway of his home! It is 6 feet 7 inches tall and 26 feet in diameter. Where do you think he parks his car?

Largest chair

You'd better sit down for this one. The world's largest chair was built in Saint Florian, Austria, in 2009. You'd need a ladder to get to the seat, as the chair is 98 feet 5 inches high!

The giant chair was made from 102 cubic yards of Douglas fir to promote a furniture store.

Longest underwater kiss

The record for the longest underwater kiss was set by Italian free divers Ilaria Bonin and Mike Maric, who puckered up for 3 minutes 8 seconds at Castelnuovo del Garda, in northern Italy in 2011.

Biggest afro

The world's biggest afro belongs to Aevin Dugas, a social worker from New Orleans. Her crowning glory has been teased to an amazing 4 feet 4 inches. Her hairdo causes a few problems when she strolls along the sidewalk, though, as it keeps getting caught in trees!

WEIRD AND AMAZING

Wheelchair users pulled a plane at Melsbroek military airport, near Brussels, in 2011.

Record plane pull

An amazing group of 84 wheelchair users broke an unusual world record when they managed to haul a C130 cargo airplane, weighing 67 tons, more than 328 feet at an airstrip in Belgium. That's wheel power!

Oldest twin sisters

The world's oldest twin sisters are Evelyn Middleton and Edith Ritchie of Scotland. These bonnie lassies were born in 1909, when William Howard Taft was President of the United States!

Most spoons on body

Here's a weird one: the record for balancing the most spoons on a human body! Kick-boxer Etibar Elchyev, of Georgia, in Eurasia, stuck 50 magnetized spoons to his neck and chest. It must be his magnetic personality that does it!

Longest dog ears

Harbor has the longest doggy ears on the planet! The eight-year-old black and tan Coonhound, who hails from Boulder, Colorado, has one ear measuring 12¼ inches and one measuring 13½ inches. The only problem, says his owner Jennifer Wert, is that he keeps tripping over them!

RECORD BREAKER

Chanel Tapper of California is the lady with the longest tongue in the world. It's 3.8 inches from end to end. Lick that!

Longest skateboard trip

The longest journey ever taken by skateboard is 7,555 miles, traveled between Lausanne in Switzerland and Shanghai in China. The champion long distance skateboarder is Robert Thompson of New Zealand.

115

WEIRD AND AMAZING

Longest bridal train

All women want to make a big impression on their wedding day. One way to do it might be to wear the dress with the world's longest bridal train. Seamstresses in Bucharest, Romania, designed a silk and lace gown with a 9,022-foot train! How many maids of honor would it take to carry that?

DID YOU KNOW? DID YOU KNOW? DID YOU KNOW? DID YOU KNOW? DID YOU KNOW?

Svetlana Pankratova, from Russia, is the lady with the world's longest legs. Her legs are 4 foot 4 inches long, and she finds it impossible to buy pants that fit!

Most walnuts crushed

Michael Levillain of Paris, France, holds the nuttiest world record yet. He crushed a line of 58 walnuts in one minute by sitting on them in 2011!

Most dogs skipping

The world record for the most dogs skipping rope is 13 pooches. It is held by Uchida Geinosha's Super Wan Wan Circus in Japan. That's barking mad!

Most door signs

Some guys just want to be left alone. Jean-François Vernetti, from Switzerland, has collected 8,888 different "Do Not Disturb" signs from hotel rooms across 189 countries since 1985. We get the message!

DO NOT DISTURB

Record bottle-top ride

Lutz Eichholz, of Germany, set a new world record by riding a **unicycle** along the top of 127 beer bottles in Tel Aviv, Israel. In an amazing display of balance, he rode the unicycle 26.21 feet and didn't break a single bottle.

WEIRD AND AMAZING

Most valuable hair

NFL star player Troy Polamalu, of the Pittsburg Steelers, has his **trademark** long, curly hair insured for a record breaking $1 million!

Most clocks

One guy who is never late for an appointment is Bill Williams from Colyton, New Zealand. Bill has 3,021 different clocks. They filled up his home until his wife persuaded him to set up a clock museum in the local church in 2005.

Longest cat
Stewie the Maine Coon is the world's longest **domestic** cat. He measures just over 4 feet from nose to tail. The gentle giant hails from Reno, Nevada.

The maple leaf is the national emblem for Canada.

Largest maple leaf
The largest maple leaf ever discovered measured an amazing 13.63 inches by 11.5 inches. It fell off a tree in Pickering, Ontario, Canada, in October 2010.

Largest pop band
The world's largest pop group is a girl band called AKB48. The group, from Tokyo, Japan, has 64 members. They also hold the record for the most singles ever sold by a female group in Japan, with nearly 12 million sales!

WEIRD AND AMAZING

Most bees

This is a record that's not for the faint-hearted! A man named Vipin Seth allowed himself to be covered in live bees in New Delhi, India, in 2009. It was calculated that 613,500 buzzing bees, weighing 136 pounds 4 ounces, swarmed all over his body.

Honey bees are attracted to the body by a queen bee.

Fastest ice cream scooper

Mitch Cohen, from Flushing, Queens, is the fastest ice cream scooper in the world! He scooped 18 rounds of ice cream into 18 cones in one minute to set a new record. This is the guy you'd want serving you on a hot day!

Lowest limbo

How low can you go? Shemika Charles, from Buffalo, New York, can limbo under a bar that's only 8.5 inches from the ground. She's the world's lowest limbo dancer.

DID YOU KNOW? DID YOU KNOW? DID YOU KNOW? DID YOU KNOW?

The longest sausage ever made was 1,738.8 feet long. It was made by a team of cooks in Vinkovic, Croatia, in 2010.

Oddest ball skills

The weird ball skills award goes to Thaneshwar Guragai, of Nepal. He spun a basketball on top of a toothbrush that he held in his mouth for 22.41 seconds!

Tiny cow

Have you ever seen a full-grown cow as small as a sheep? Swallow, a Dexter breed cow from Cheshire, UK, stands just 2 feet 7.5 inches tall. She lives on a farm, where she has already given birth to ten regular-size calves.

WEIRD AND AMAZING

Extreme rope walk

It takes guts and amazing balance to attempt an aerial tightrope walk, but stuntman Samat Hasan took it to the next level. He walked along a 2,300-foot rope, angled 39° uphill, in Hunan Province, China, to clinch a new world record.

Samat Hasan wore rubber boots to grip the 1.2-inch wire.

Longest hike with fridge

Most people pack fresh clothes and a tent when they set off on a hike. British comedian Tony Hawks decided to take a small fridge with him when he hitchhiked across Ireland in 1997. The trip covered 1,025 miles and earned him the world record for "longest distance traveled with a fridge!"

TONY HAWKS

THE FRIDGE-HIKER'S GUIDE TO LIFE

Record fruit roll

Ashrita Furman took his love of fruit to a new extreme when he rolled an orange almost one mile across Terminal 4 at JFK Airport, New York...with his nose! It took him 29 minutes and set a new, weird world record!

DID YOU KNOW? DID YOU KNOW? DID YOU KNOW? DID YOU KNOW?

The shortest commercial air flight in the world takes just two minutes to fly 8.6 miles between the islands of Papa Westray and Westray in the Scottish Orkney isles.

Most eggs balanced

The world record for balancing the most eggs on their ends is held by Brian Spotts of Dacono, Colorado. He managed to stand 900 eggs on end in Hong Kong, China, in 2011. Eggs-actly how did he do that?

Sneezing record

In 1981, 12-year-old Donna Griffiths of Worcestershire, England, woke up and sneezed. She didn't stop sneezing for 944 days straight—that's more than two and a half years and a sneezing world record!

123

KNOCKOUT SPORTS

Bei-jing's 91,000-seater "Bird's Nest" stadium includes a hotel and an underground shopping mall.

Most expensive Olympics

The most expensive Olympic Games ever staged took place in Beijing, China, in 2008. The Chinese hosts spent $43 billion on the event and got the biggest television audience ever for a sports event. More than 4.7 billion people watched the Olympics on TV, which equals to two people out of every three in the entire world!

DID YOU KNOW? DID YOU KNOW? DID YOU KNOW? DID YOU KNOW?

The very first Olympic record was set by a long-jump athlete from Sparta, in Ancient Greece, in 656 B.C.E. His name was Chionis and he jumped 21 feet. That's still pretty impressive today!

First perfect ten

Nadia Comaneci of Romania was the first gymnast to score a perfect ten at the Olympics. She got the score for her routine on the bars at the Montreal Olympics in 1976. She went on to win three gold medals at the event...and she was just 14 years old!

Greatest Olympian

Michael Phelps, from Baltimore, Maryland is the greatest **Olympian** of all time. The swimmer won a record-breaking 22 medals (18 gold, two silver, two bronze) between 2004 and 2012.

Most medals won for the U.S.

Michael Phelps also holds the record for the most Olympic gold medals ever won by a U.S. competitor. Phelps won six gold medals at the Athens Olympics in 2004, eight in Beijing in 2008, and four in London in 2012. Eight gold medals is also the most ever won by an athlete at a single Olympic Games!

KNOCKOUT SPORTS

Top player

Jerry Rice is the greatest football wide receiver of all time, so it was no surprise when he was named the NFL's "Top Player of All Time" in 2010. Jerry holds every major receiving record as well as the most all-time yards and touchdowns.

Jerry Rice played for the San Francisco 49ers, the Oakland Raiders, and the Seattle Seahawks.

Most interceptions

Football defensive back Paul Krause holds the all-time NFL record for the most interceptions with 81, which he returned for 1,185 yards and three touchdowns.

Record breaking quarterback

Record breaking former quarterback and passing **supremo** Dan Marino can boast totals of 61,361 yards, 8,358 attempts, 4,967 completions, and 420 touchdowns during his 16-year **career** with the Miami Dolphins.

Award winner

Emmitt Smith is the National Football League's all-time rushing yards leader, gaining 18,355 yards in his long career. He is the only running back to have won the Superbowl Championship, Superbowl Most Valuable Player, NFL Most Valuable Player, and NFL Rushing Crown awards all in the same season (with the Dallas Cowboys in 1993).

DID YOU KNOW? DID YOU KNOW? DID YOU KNOW? DID YOU KNOW?

Kicker Gary Anderson holds the record for the most field goal points scored in a lifetime, with 2,434 between 1982 and 2004. He was the first NFL kicker to score a perfect season, scoring 94 field goals from 94 kicks in 1998.

Most sacks

Sack leader Bruce Smith is one of the best NFL defense players of all time. His record of 200 career sacks has not been beat. His 13 professional seasons with ten or more sacks is also an NFL record.

KNOCKOUT SPORTS

First F1 champ

The world's first ever Formula 1 champion was the Italian driver Giuseppe Farina, who won the prize for his team, Alpha Romeo, in 1950 at the age of 44.

Michael (driving here for Ferrari) and Ralf Schumacher are the only brothers to win F1 races.

Largest points lead

Ferrari driver Michael Schumacher had the largest points lead in the history of Formula 1 Motor Racing in 2002, when he finished 67 points in front of his teammate Rubens Barrichello to win the Formula 1 Championship. This German driver also has the record for winning the most F1 Championships. He has won seven times!

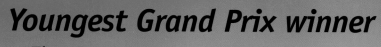

Youngest Grand Prix winner

The youngest-ever Grand Prix winner is Sebastian Vettel of Germany, who won the 2008 Italian F1 Championship for his team, Toro Rosso, over 53 laps at the Monza racetrack. He was just 21 years old!

Only father and son winners

British racing drivers Graham and Damon Hill are the only father and son to have won the Formula 1 trophy. Dad Graham won twice: in 1962, driving for BRM, and in 1968 for the Lotus team; his son Damon won in 1996 for the Williams team.

Constructor's record

The Ferrari motor team, from Italy, has won the Formula 1 Championship more times than any other car constructor, with a record-breaking 16 wins.

KNOCKOUT SPORTS

Grand Slam record

Rod Laver, from Australia, holds the record for winning twice the tennis Grand Slam, which is the Australian Open, the French Open, Wimbledon (UK), and the U.S. Open. He won all four tournaments in 1962 and 1969.

Most female winners

The USA has had more female world tennis champions than any other country, with a record breaking eight winners. They are: Chris Evert, Martina Navratilova, Tracy Austin, Monica Seles, Lindsay Davenport, Jennifer Capriati, and the Williams sisters, Venus and Serena. That's girl power!

Longest at number one

U.S. tennis player Pancho Gonzales was the world's number one for a record eight years in the 1950s and 1960s. He got interested in tennis when his mom gave him a 51-cent racket when he was 12 years old!

Youngest Grand Slam champ

The youngest man ever to win the world tennis Grand Slam is Spain's Rafael Nadal. He was just 21 when he won all four tournaments in 2010. He is a left-handed tennis player but he writes with his right hand!

Nadal is nicknamed "The King of Clay" due to his success on clay courts.

Longest match

The longest professional tennis match ever played lasted 11 hours and five minutes! The record-breaking match was between Nicolas Mahut of France and John Isner of the USA. It happened at Wimbledon, UK, between June 22–24, 2010.

KNOCKOUT SPORTS

Fastest 400 meters

Retired U.S. sprinter Michael Johnson still holds the world and Olympic records for the fastest 400 **meters** (43.18 seconds) and, with his teammates, the fastest 400-meter relay (two minutes, 54.29 seconds). He was famous for running upright and raising his knees high. It must have worked, as he was the world's fastest man until Usain Bolt came along!

Fastest runner

The fastest man in the world today is the Jamaican runner Usain Bolt. He smashed his own Olympic 100-meter **sprint** record of 9.69 seconds in 2009, crossing the tape in 9.58 seconds. He did the same with his 200-meter record, getting that down to 19.19 seconds. His speed has earned him the nickname "Lightning Bolt!"

Fastest mile

The fastest mile ever run took three minutes 43.13 seconds. The runner was Hicham El Guerrouj of Morocco, in northern Africa. He began his sporting career as a goalkeeper for his local soccer team. It's just as well he gave it up, as there's not much running involved in goalkeeping!

DID YOU KNOW? DID YOU KNOW? DID YOU KNOW? DID YOU KNOW?

The world's fastest ever woman was the athlete Florence Griffith-Joyner, from Los Angeles, California. Her 100-meter sprint in 10.49 seconds has not been beaten since she passed away in 1998.

Fastest marathon

Running a marathon of 26 miles, 365 yards is a big deal. Kenyan runner Patrick Makau Musyoki takes it all in stride as he is the world's fastest ever marathon runner. He completed the 2011 Berlin Marathon in Germany in a record breaking two hours, three minutes, 38 seconds!

KNOCKOUT SPORTS

RBI record

Making the hit that produces base runners is key in baseball. The top run-batted-in player of all time is Hank Aaron, whose RBI record is an amazing 2,297. "Hammerin' Hank" played 21 seasons with the Milwaukee and the Atlanta Braves between 1954 and 1974.

Most games

The Major League Baseball player who played in the most games during his professional career was Pete Rose. The switch hitter turned in 3,562 appearances between 1963 and 1986, wearing the number 14 jersey for the Cincinnati Reds, the Philadelphia Phillies, and the Montreal Expos. He also logged the most hits in baseball, with an astounding 4,256.

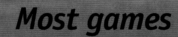

Most career home runs

Nothing gets baseball fans on their feet like a long ball!
The record for scoring the most career home runs belongs to
Barry Bonds, who scored 762. He played for the Pittsburgh
Pirates from 1986 to 1992, switching to the San Francisco
Giants until he left in 2007.

RECORD BREAKER

Left fielder Rickey
Henderson is the
lifetime base thief in the
history of MLB. He played
for nine teams between 1979
and 2003 and stole 1,406
bases, which is still a
baseball record!

Highest batting average

The highest lifetime batting average
is held by center fielder Ty Cobb, who
played for the Detroit Tigers (1905–
1926) and the Philadelphia
Athletics (1927–1928).
Nicknamed "The Georgia
Peach," his batting
average was .367, which
is still the MLB record.
Many experts think
his batting average
will never
be beaten!

EXTREME SPORTS

Glenn Singleman and Heather Swan soared down from Meru Peak after a tough 22-day climb in sub-zero conditions.

Highest BASE jump

The world's highest BASE jump took place from the top of Mount Meru in India in 2006. Australian couple, Glenn Singleman and Heather Swan, jumped off a cliff edge at 21,666 feet and floated to the ground using wingsuits and parachutes.

Horse versus Man Marathon winners

In the tiny town of Llanwrtyd Wells in Wales, UK, a "Horse versus Man Marathon" race has happened every year since 1980! Only two men have ever managed to beat the horses, running over 22 miles of rough countryside: Huw Lobb of London, UK, in 2004, and Florian Holzinger of Germany, in 2007. Talk about horsepower!

Longest sled-dog race

The longest sled-dog race on Earth covers 1,049 icy miles across Alaska. The temperature can dip below -100°F, but competitors in the Iditarod Trail Race don't stick around to worry about it. The fastest time taken to finish the race is eight days, 18 hours, and 46 minutes by dog musher John Baker of Kotzebue, Alaska, in 2011.

DID YOU KNOW? DID YOU KNOW? DID YOU KNOW? DID YOU KNOW?

A Las Vegas teenager who has **spina bifida** became the first person ever to do a backflip in a wheelchair in 2008. Record breaker Aaron Fotheringham calls the sport "hardcore sitting!"

Fastest road race

The fastest road race in the world is the Silver State Classic Challenge, which takes place on Route 318 in Nevada. Drivers average 190 miles per hour as they race 90 miles toward the finish line. It's the real Wacky Races!

GLOSSARY

Altitude
The height of something, such as an airplane in the sky or a mountain.

Amass
To gather or collect something.

Asteroid
A small mass that orbits the sun that is not large enough to be a planet.

Auction
A sale where things are sold to the person who offers the most money.

B.C.E
Three letters that appear after a date to explain how many years before the common era an event happened; so 7th century B.C.E means 700 years before the common era.

Bizarre
Something very strange or unusual.

Carat
The weight of jewels or gold; 1 carat = .007 ounces

Career
A job that a person does for a long time.

C.E
Two letters that appear after a date to explain how many years after the common era an event happened.

Checkmate
A move in a game of chess that means one player loses because their "king" chess piece cannot move from their current position on the board.

Choreographer
A person who tells dancers how they should move in a particular dance.

Animal with the most teeth
Page 20

Continent
A huge piece of land surrounded by ocean. North America, Africa, Asia, and Europe are all continents.

Contorted
Twisted into an unusual or uncomfortable shape.

Crustacean
A creature that has a hard shell, such as a crab or a lobster.

Decibel
How sound is measured; your ears can begin to hurt if a noise is above 85 decibels.

Dedication
Being loyal and sticking at something, such as a job.

Diameter
A straight line through the center of a circle, from one side to the other.

Dictionary
A book that lists the meanings of words in alphabetical order, from a to z.

Domestic
In this example, a tame animal or pet that lives with its owners.

Eccentric
A person who is a bit unusual or quirky.

Edible
Safe to eat.

Epic
Large or impressive and usually quite difficult to achieve.

Equivalent
Equal to (=), or having the same value as something else.

Extraterrestrial
Any life that exists in space or on another planet.

Extravagant
Very fancy or expensive or generous.

Fastest feet
Page 26

Feat
A big achievement or an act that requires great skill.

Fossil
The skeleton of an animal or plant that lived a long time ago that you can see embedded in a rock.

Franchise
Giving or having permission to sell someone else's products or services.

Gamma-ray
Powerful invisible rays from space.

Gravity
The invisible natural force that keeps our feet touching the ground and causes things to fall down towards Earth instead of floating upwards into space.

Hercules
A hero in ancient times who supposedly had superhuman strength.

Hourglass
A tool used to measure time. It has an upper and lower glass bulb with a very narrow "waist" in the middle, through which sand slowly trickles from the top bulb into the bottom one. When there is no more sand in the top bulb, an hour has passed.

GLOSSARY

Impact
What happens when one thing strikes another.

Invasion
The act of entering a place without being invited.

Licensed
Having official permission to use someone else's idea or product.

Memorabilia
A collection of items related to a particular person or event or thing, for example, Donald Duck or Star Wars.

Meteor
A lump of burning rock or metal that falls to Earth from space.

Meter
A metric measurement.
1 meter = 3.28 feet

Migration
When animals or birds move to a different place at certain times of the year.

Miniature
Small or tiny.

Miser
A mean person who doesn't like spending their money even though they might have plenty.

Monsoon
Very heavy rainfall that occurs in parts of Asia in summer.

Myth
A traditional story that may be true or made up.

Navigate
To find the way to a place.

Olympian
An athlete who has taken part in the Olympics.

Plasma
In this example, small clouds of gas that can conduct electricity and which float in space.

Plectrum
A small, thin piece of plastic or metal that is used to strum the strings of a guitar.

Plummet
To fall straight down, suddenly and very quickly.

Population
The total number of people in an area.

Radar
Electronic equipment that uses radio waves to detect the position of objects that are far away.

Reign
The period during which a king or queen is ruler of a kingdom.

Scorched
Burned or withered by intense heat.

Sheer
In this example, it means transparent (see-through).

Fastest police
Page 25

Slither
To slide along the ground, the way a snake moves.

Solar System
In this example, the 8 planets, including Earth, plus their moons, asteroids, and space debris that orbit (go around) our Sun.

Species
A group of living things with similar features. Humans are one species, while dogs, horses, and apes are each a different type of species.

Spina Bifida
A medical condition whereby a person's spine (backbone) hasn't formed properly. This might mean that they can't move their muscles the same way other people do.

Sprint
To run at top speed for a short distance.

Supersonic
Faster than the speed of sound. The speed of sound travels at 1,108 feet (337.3 m) per second.

Supremo
The person with the highest rank or most qualifications.

Sushi
Japanese finger food: shaped, cooked rice that usually has a topping of raw fish.

Trademark
In this example, a distinctive feature that you would associate with a person, such as long, curly hair.

Tribal
Belonging to a particular tribe or group of people.

Twitter
In this example, a very popular system that allows people to send short, instant text messages on a mobile phone to a group of people (called "followers").

Tyrannosaur
A large meat-eating dinosaur with short arms and legs and a huge head with sharp teeth. T-rex was the largest known tyrannosaur.

Unicycle
A form of pedal-powered transport that has a cycle saddle balanced above just one wheel.

Unmanned
Without a driver, pilot, or crew; operated by a remote or automatic control.

Volume
In this example, it means size.

Wall Street
The area of New York City where the financial business of the United States is controlled.

Tallest man alive
Page 10

INDEX

Heaviest insect
Page 18

INDEX